The Ultimate eBook Creator

SERGEY SKUDAEV

CONTENTS

SERGEY SKUDAEV

1. Who is this Book for?

This book is intended for self-publishing authors who plan to publish their books on their own, without resorting to traditional publishers. It is assumed that readers can use a computer, although they are not experts. For each step, there is a screenshot and explanations, so anyone who really wants to learn how to make an e-book can learn this. Yes, it will take some effort from you to understand the technical details.

There are many formats of e-books, but you need to master only one format - EPUB. All other formats can be converted from the EPUB format automatically. Therefore, the EPUB format should be perfect. And for this you need to learn how to edit it manually. You will need some knowledge of HTML and CSS scripts, which are used to make websites. But do not be alarmed. I have provided you with all the steps you may need to create your book.

Today, there are many companies that provide authors with the opportunity to publish their books on their own. The largest company that provides authors with the opportunity to self-publish their books is Amazon.

If you are not a writer, but a business owner, then you can write and publish a book in order to show that you are an expert in your field, as well as to advertise your brand.

In Europe, you can publish your book on Streetlib.com.

In Canada, there is a site, https://www.kobo.com/us/en/p/writinglife.

In the United States, you can publish your book on https://www.smashwords.com and barnesandnoble.com/b/nook-books/. You can publish your eBook on Google Play: http://play.google.com/books/publish/

All these companies allow authors to publish books for free in different languages. They not only sell e-books, but also distribute them through other online stores. Authors are paid about 70% of the cost of the eBook. Even if you are not going to write books, you can learn how to make electronic books in order to earn money.

In the USA, converting an MS Word document to the EPUB format costs $ 150.

There are sites (Free and Paid) that promote the books:

1) Best Reads: https://bestreads.app
2) WordLikes: https://wordlikes.com
3) BMI Books: https://bmibooks.com (Starting from $10 onetime fee)
4) Writers Support: https://writers.support
5) WriteGlobe: https://writeglobe.com
6) Creative Designers Writers(Free): https://creativedesignerswriters.com
7) OltoApp: https://olto.app (Free and Paid)
8) BooksWi-Fi: https://bookswifi.com
9) Olto Books: https://oltobooks.com/
10) Free99Books: https://free99books.com
11) Free-eBooks: https://www.free-ebooks.net/1250ebooks
12) Bookbub: https://bookbub.com
13) BookBaby: https://bookbaby.com
14) https://www.booksbutterfly.com/

You can download the demo eBook "Lost in The Fall" in epub, mobi and print on demand format here:
http://learn-coding.today/epub/fall.zip

2 How to Make a Cover for Your Book

A book begins with a cover! All successful book authors and marketers claim that a book is judged by its cover. Successful writers spend hundreds of dollars on a book cover.

In the United States, a cover design costs a minimum of $ 199. But you can find a cheaper designer at Fiverr: http://fiverr.com or Upwork: https://www.upwork.com/cat/designers/. There you can make a cover for $ 10-20. But you must understand that you get what you pay for.

If you have a talent for design, you can make the cover yourself and I will teach you how, although I do not have designer's talent. I just know how to use the applications necessary for making covers.

For the cover you need an illustration or photograph of at least 1600 x 2500 pixels.

If you do not have a suitable photo, you can find it on pixabay.com. On this site, all photos and illustrations are royalty free. To search for photos, enter keywords and a size greater than 5000 pixels and click Go. (Fig. 1)

Figure 1. Pixabay.com website. Search Photos.

Click on the image you like and the "Free Download" button will appear on the right. (Fig. 2)

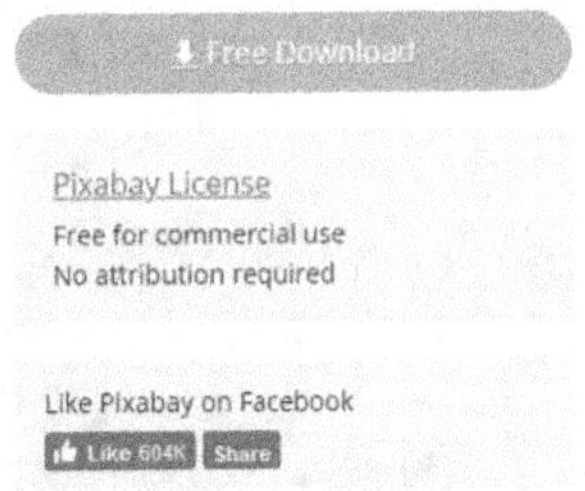

Figure 2. Pixabay.com License.

It is very important to make sure that the author of the image allows you to use it for commercial purposes and does not require an indication of its authorship. That is - Free for commercial use No attribution required.

Click on the "Free Download" button, select the maximum size and save the image on your computer. (Fig. 3)

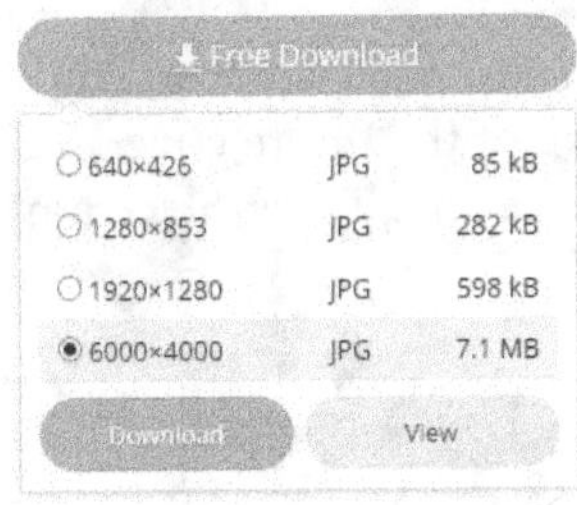

Figure 3. Select the maximum image size.

Why do I need to search for photos larger than 5000 pixels and download an image of maximum size?

The fact is that photos for the cover and for illustrations inside the book should be 300 dpi or at least 200 dpi.

DPI means dot per inch. Most free photos have 96 dpi. If an image with a size of 6000 pixels and 96 dpi "is squeezed" three times, then the number of dots per inch will increase 3 times and will be 96 x 3 = 288 dpi.

In addition, some large photos already have 300 dpi. The larger the photograph, the more likely it is to be taken with a good camera that takes photographs with a resolution of 300 dpi.

How to determine the resolution of a photograph? Right click on the file. A menu will appear. Select Properties, then select the Details tab. (Fig. 4).

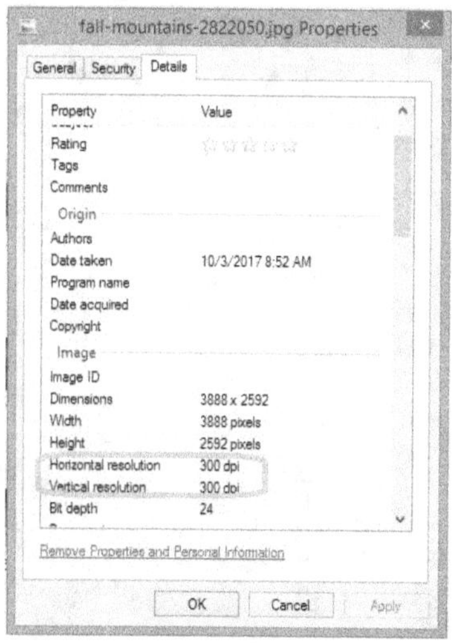

Figure 4. The resolution of the photograph is 300 dpi.

Most photos have a width greater than the height, so to make a cover, you need to cut a rectangle from the image to fit the size of the future cover. To do this, in the GIMP program, select from the main menu: Tools, Selection Tools Rectangle Select. (Fig. 5)

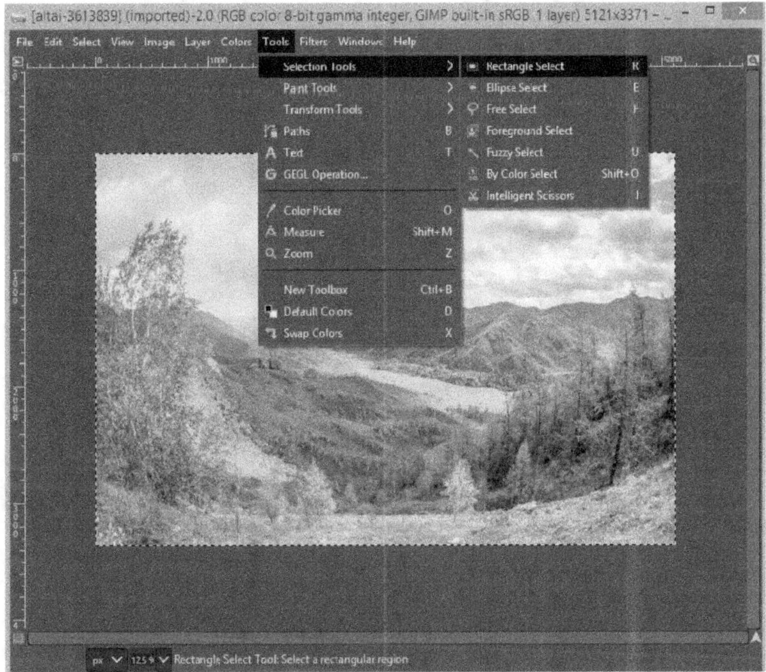

Figure 5. Selection Tools.

Select the desired rectangle with the mouse. (Fig. 6)

Figure 6. Create a rectangle that has a width to height ration of about 0.67.

Note that the task bar shows the size of the selected rectangle: 2312 x 3360 pixels. Right click on the selected rectangle and select Edit, Copy. (Fig. 7)

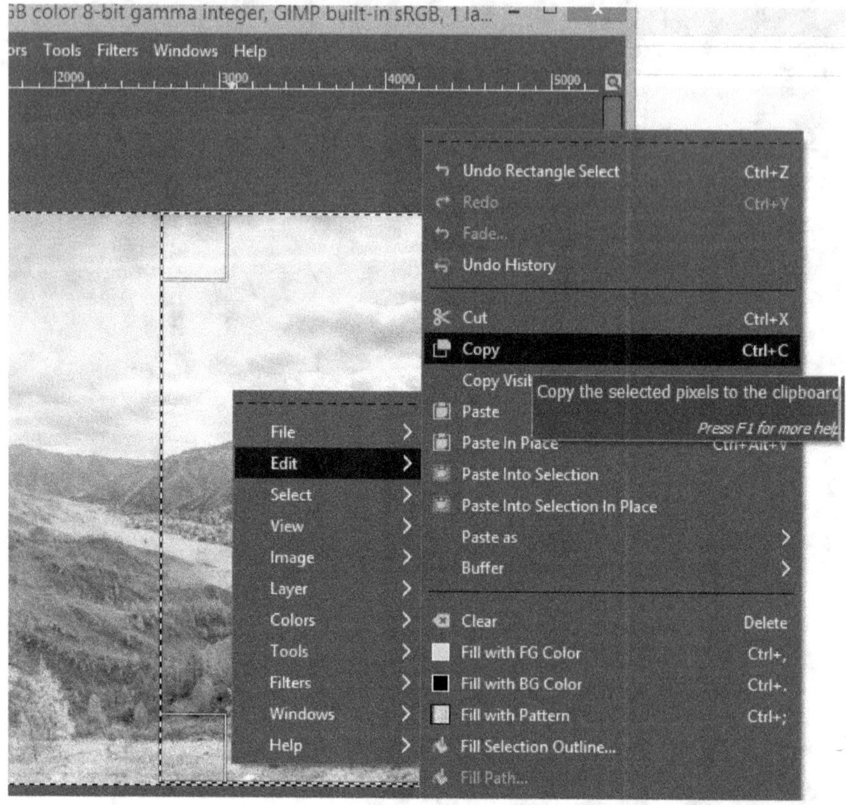

Figure 7.Copy the cover rectangle to the clipboard.

Select File, New and a window to create a new image is displayed.
(Fig. 8)

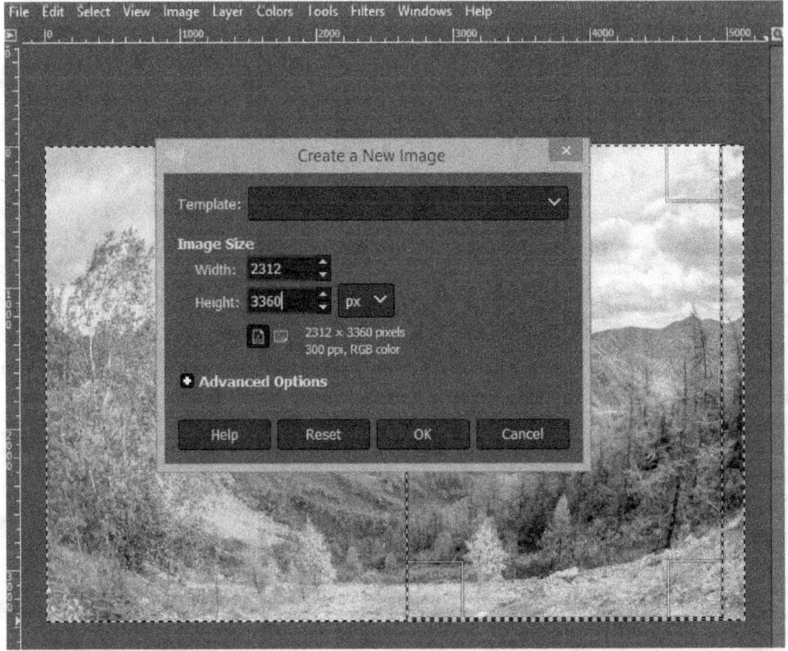

Figure 8. File, New.

Create an empty rectangle the same size as the selected rectangle for the cover. (Fig. 9)

Figure 9. The empty rectangle is created.

Right click on the empty rectangle and select Edit, Paste. (Fig. 10)

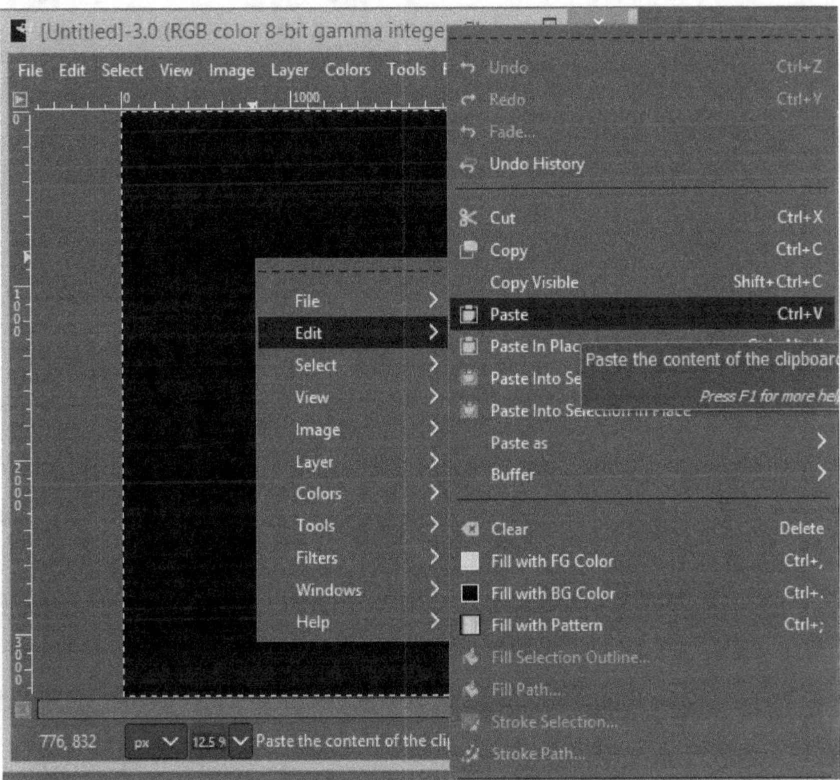

Figure 10. Edit, Paste.

Your cover image is inserted into the empty rectangle image. (Fig. 11)

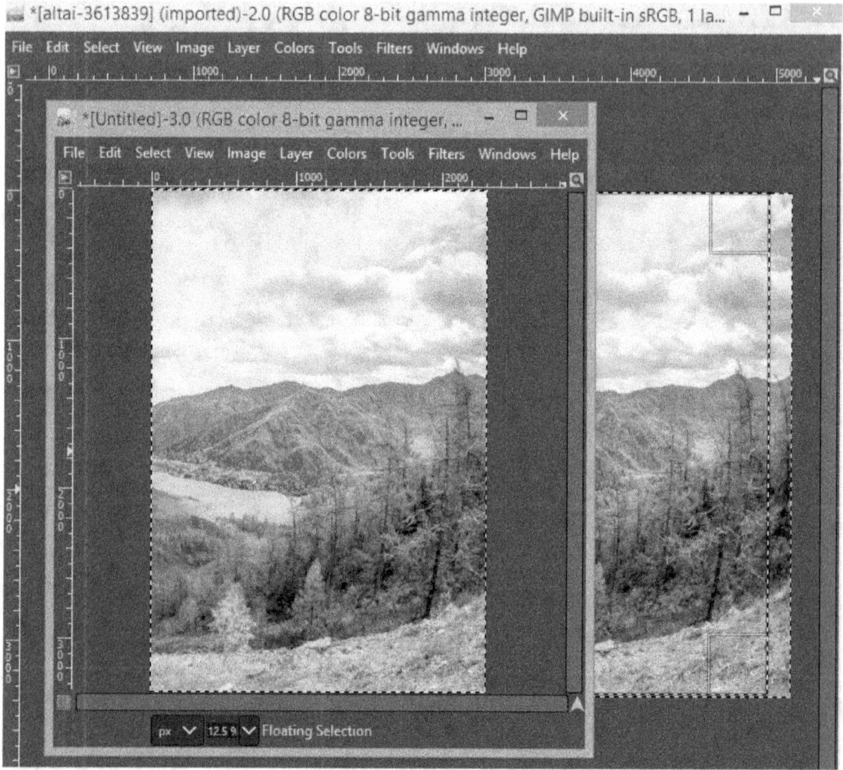

Figure 11 The copied cover image fills the empty image.

To save the image, from main menu, select File, Export As. (Fig. 12)

Figure 12. Export As.

On the next window, enter cover.jpg for the cover image name, select Jpeg for the image type and click the Export button. (Fig. 13)

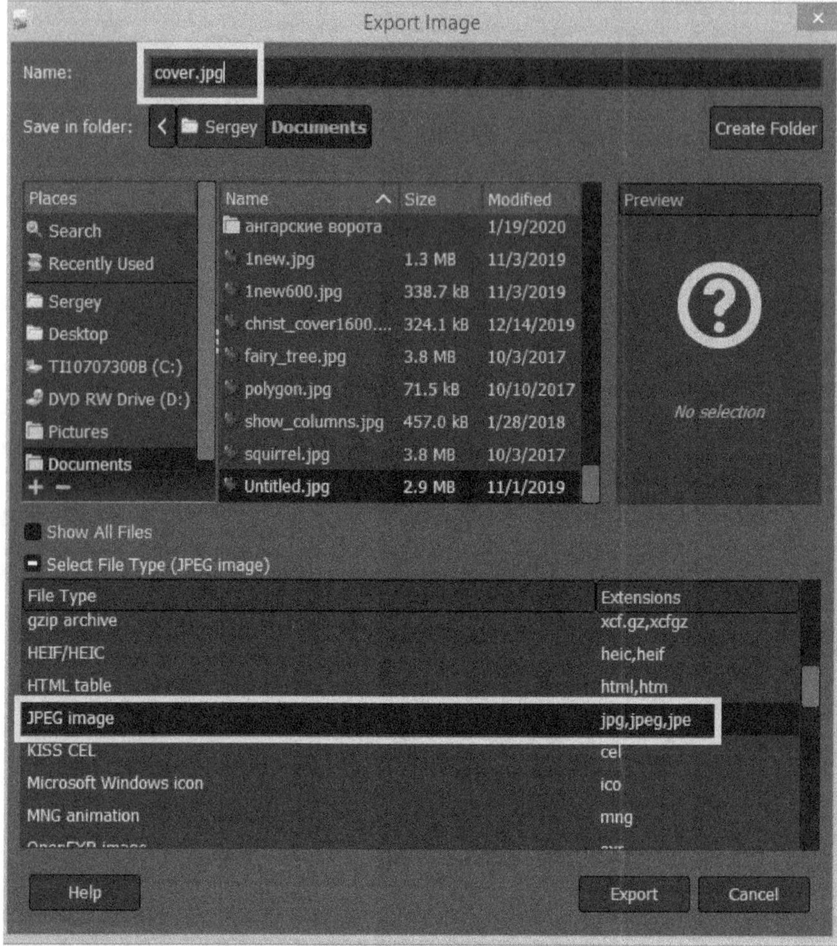

Figure 13. Export image as JPEG.

On the next window, set the quality of the image to maximum and click the Export button. (Fig 14)

Figure 14. Export Image.

Figure 15. The image is saved.

Now you have to change its size to 1600 X 2400.

Select Image, Scale Image (Fig. 16)

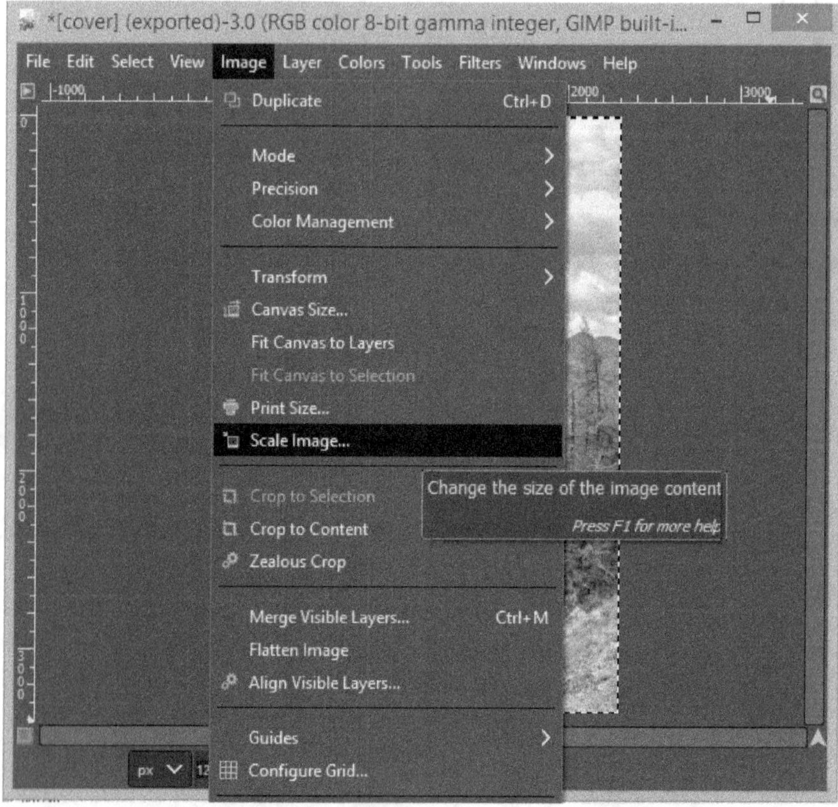

Figure 16. Scale image.

On the next window set image size to 1600 x 2400. (Fig. 17)

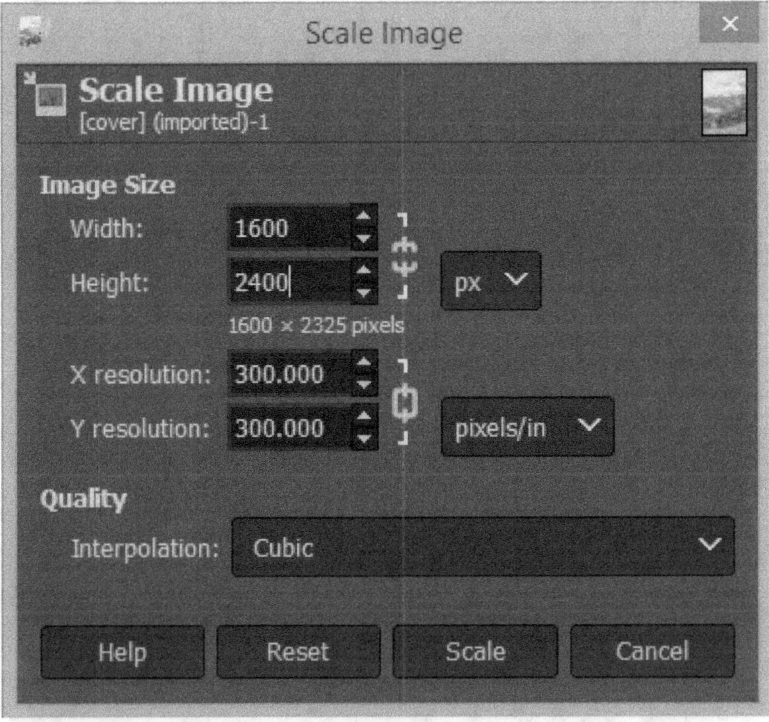

Figure 17. New image size 1600x2400.

Click the Scale button. The image size is changed. (Fig.18)

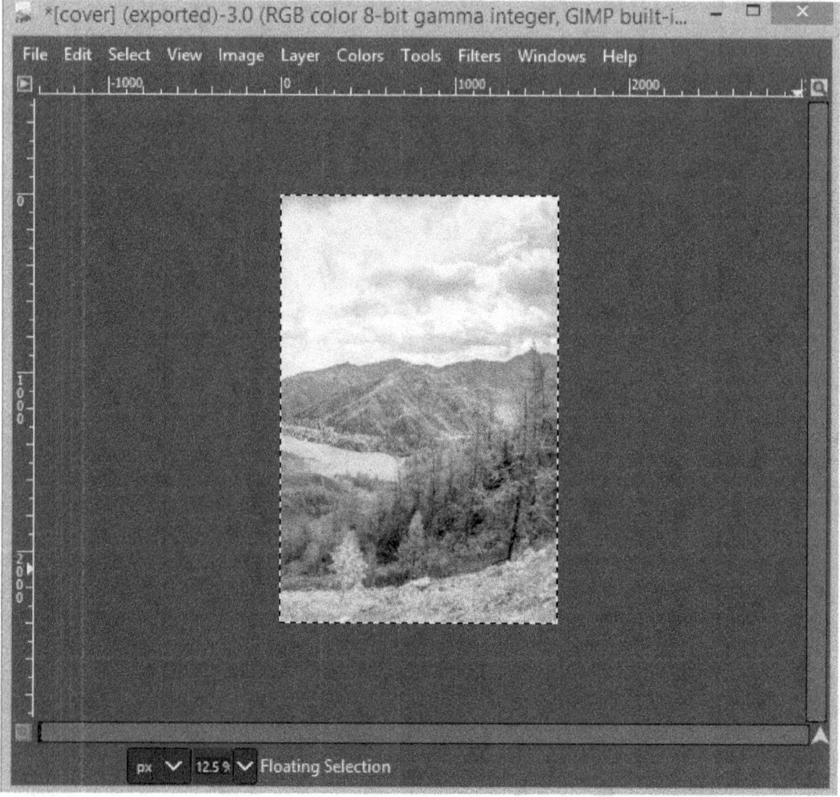

Figure 18. Image size is scaled.

To save the scaled image, select File, Export As and save the image as you did before.

3. How to Print the Title of the Book on the Book Cover

It's very convenient to use the Canva.com website for a book cover design.

They have a free plan and a paid plan of $ 12.95 per month. A free plan is enough for you.

To use the website, you need to choose a free plan and create your account. (Fig. 19)

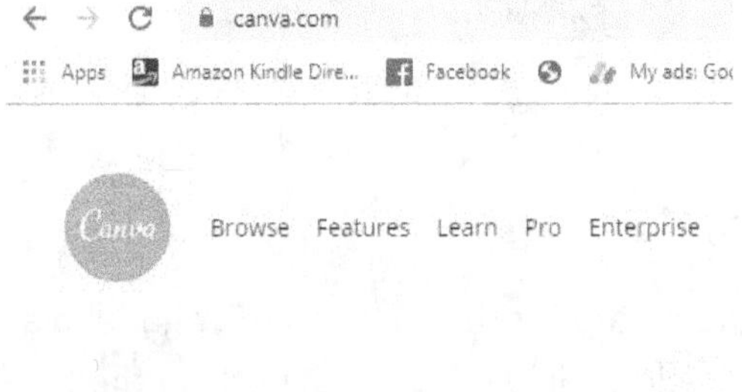

Figure 19. Canva.com website.

To create a cover, click the Create a design button. A menu will be displayed. Select the Book Cover. (Fig. 20)

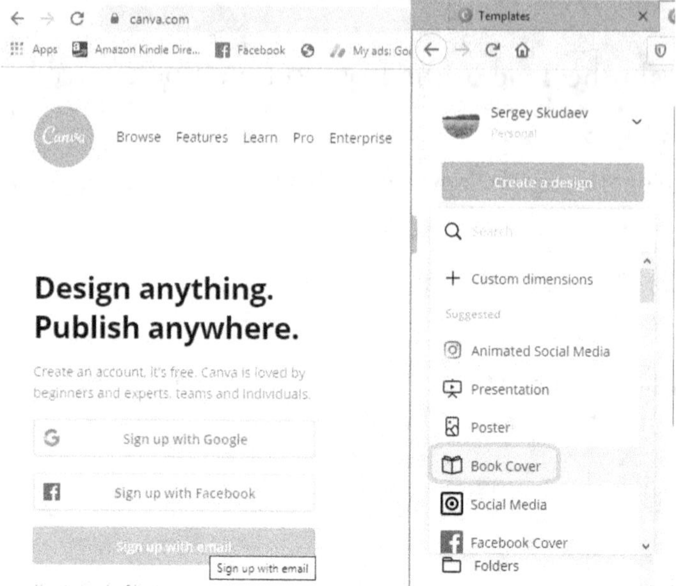

Figure 20. Menu. The Book Cover.

On the next web page, a blank template for the cover on the right and a panel with the design tools on the left will be displayed. Click on the "Upload" icon. (Fig. 21)

Figure 21. Web page with cover design tools.

Figure 22. "Upload an Image" button.

Click the "Upload an Image" button. A window for selecting an image will open. (Fig. 23)

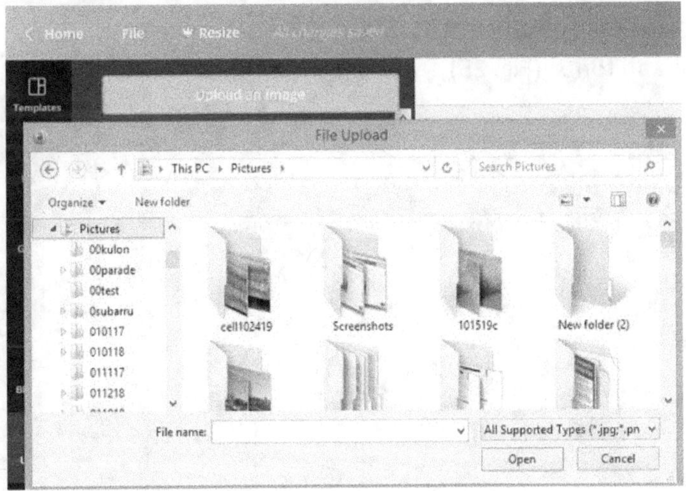

Figure 23. Window for selecting an image.

Select the desired image and it will appear under the "Upload Image" button. Click on it with the mouse and drag the image onto the blank template.

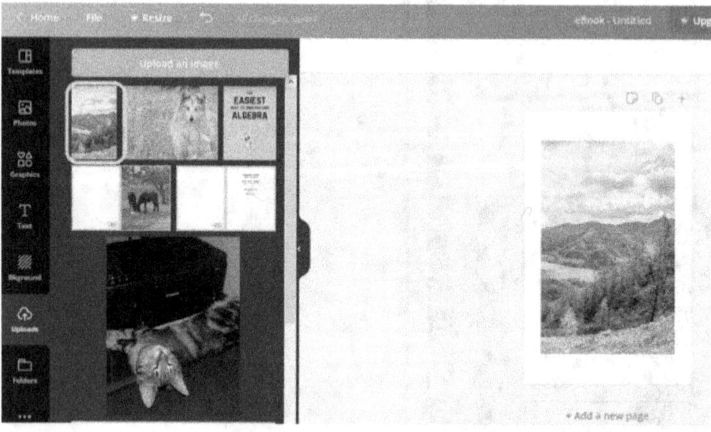

Figure 24. Adding an image to the cover template.

To add the author and title of the book, click the T - text icon. Book titles in various formats and fonts will be displayed. Here you can select a desired format and fonts. (Fig. 25)

Figure 25. Book titles in various formats.

Choose the format and fonts that are more suitable for the genre of your book and click on it with the mouse.

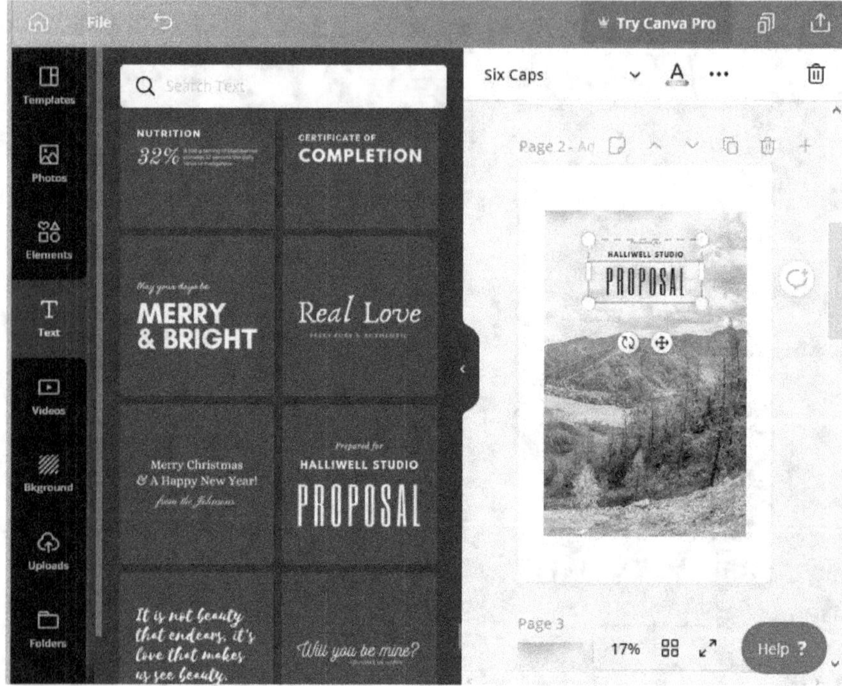

Figure 26. Selecting a title format.

Place the cursor on the text and erase the text by pressing the Delete or Backspace key on your keyboard. Next, type in the title of your book and the name of the author. (Fig. 27)

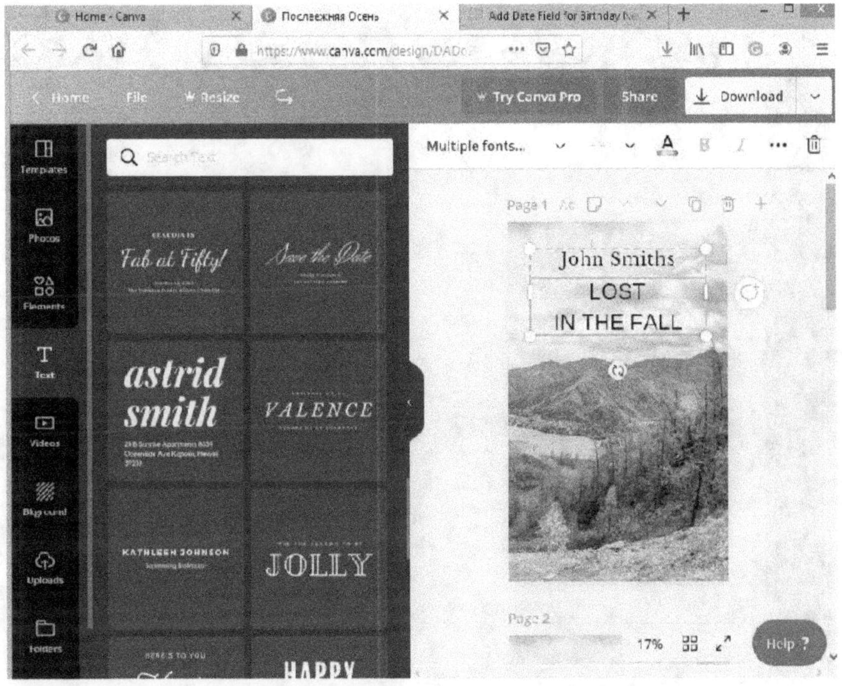

Figure 27. Replacing the original title with your title.

You can change the fonts, size and color of the text using the menu above the cover. (Fig. 28)

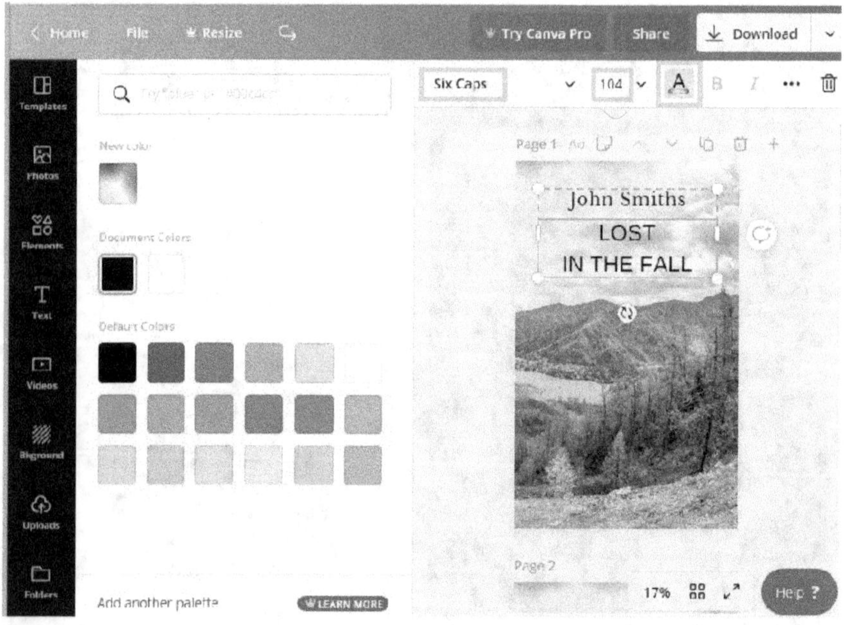

Figure 28. Changing the size and color of your fonts.

To download the finished cover, click Download. You can select JPG as the format, but then the cover resolution will be 96 dpi. If you want to keep the cover with a high resolution of 300 dpi, then you need to choose the PDF Print format. (Fig. 29)

Figure 29. Saving the cover in different formats.

It's best to make several cover options to show them to potential readers and choose the one you like best. To copy the cover, click the "Copy page" icon. (Fig. 30)

Figure 30. Copying the cover.

A new copy of the cover appears below the original. (Fig. 31).

Figure 31. Copy of the cover.

Click the title of the book on the image and press the Delete key. Repeat if necessary to remove all text. In the left pane, select a different format for the title and click it. The title will appear on the cover. (Fig. 32)

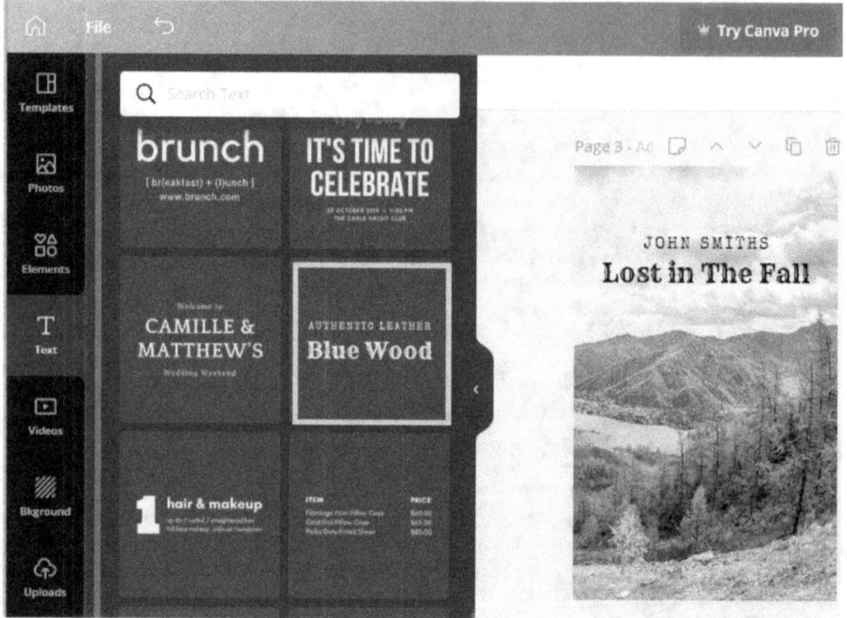

Figure 32. The title of the book in a new format.

Click the copy icon again to copy the cover and create the third cover option.

Insert a new title format into the third cover. Erase the title text on the cover and type in your title and author name. Download all your covers as the PDF Print quality. (Fig.33)

Figure 33. All three covers.

I am not a designer. I am just showing you the idea. Select the cover that looks best. A cover of 1600 x 2500 pixels is needed for the web page on which the book will be displayed for sale. But for an EPUB file, you need a cover with a width of 600-800 pixels. You can make a small cover from a large one in the GIMP program. You already know how. On the main menu, select Image, Scale image. See Figures 5, 6, 7, 8, and 9.

You downloaded a high resolution 300 dpi cover art in PDF Print format.

Now you need to convert the PDF file to a JPEG file. This can be done in the GIMP program. Choose File, Open from the menu and select a cover in PDF format. (Fig. 34)

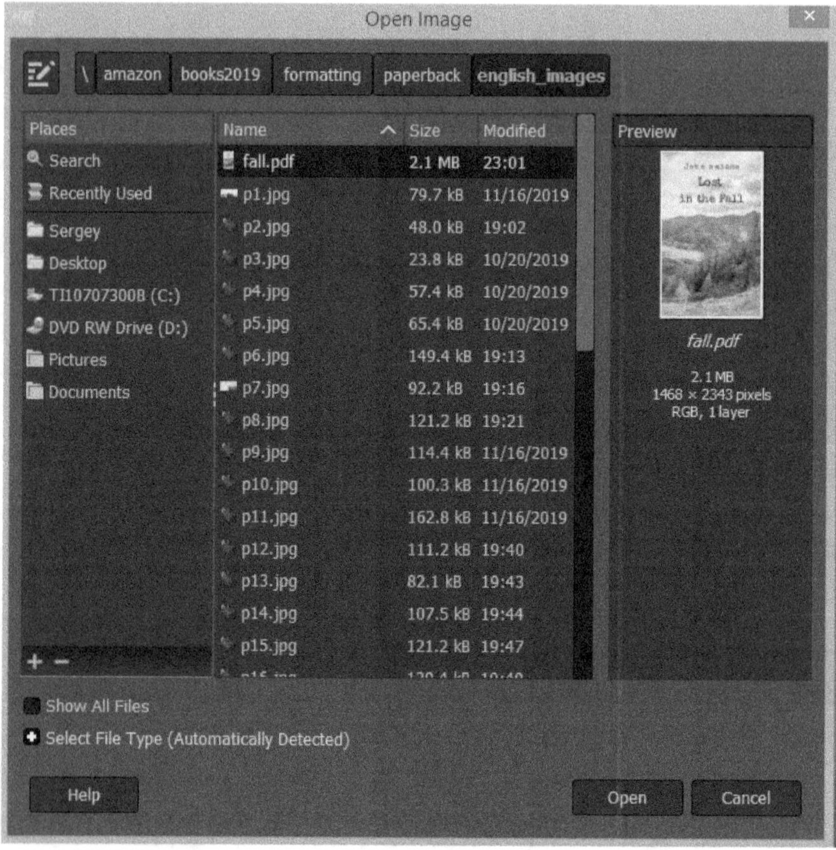

Figure 34. Select a cover in PDF format and click the Open button.

On the next window, adjust the resolution to 300 pixels. (Fig. 35)

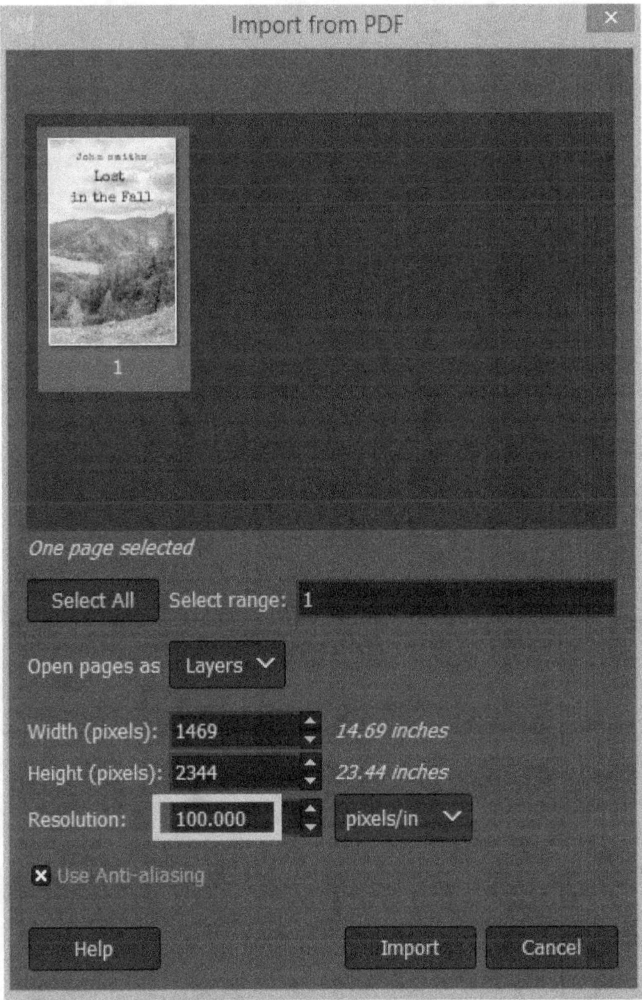

Figure 35. Import from PDF.

Note that when you change the resolution, the size of the image will be increased to 4406x7031 pixels. (Fig. 36)

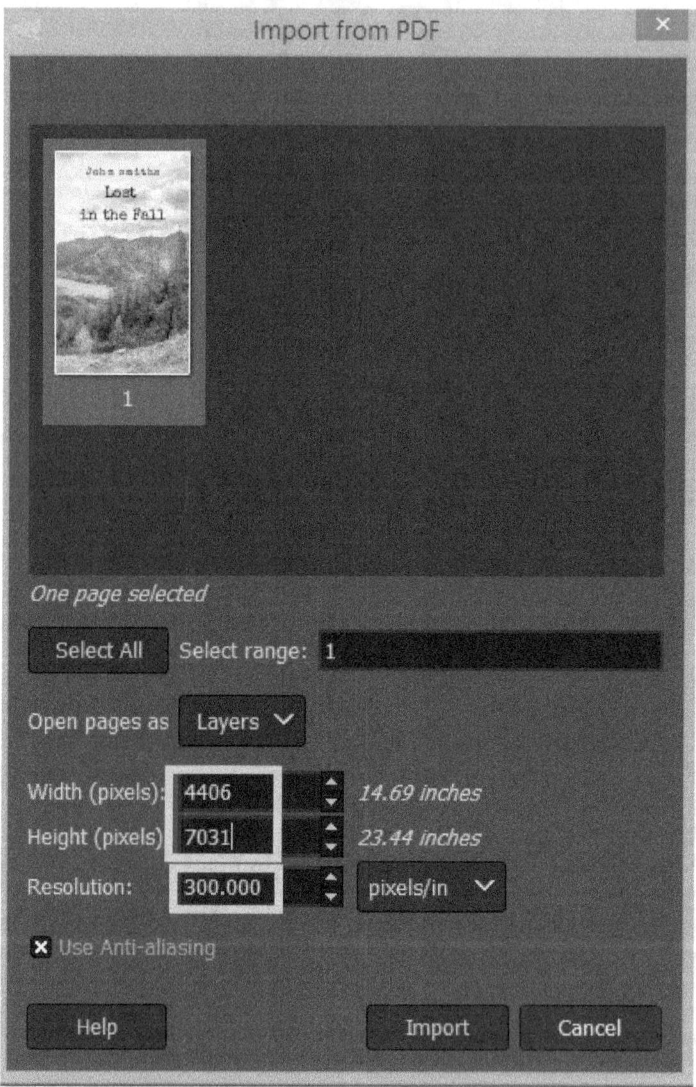

Figure 36. When the resolution is changed to 300 pixels, the size of the image is increased.

Click the Import button. The cover opens in GIMP. To resize the cover image back to 1600x2500 pixels, select Image, Scale Image from the main menu. Click the Scale button (Fig. 37).

Figure 37. Scale Image in GIMP

To save the file as a jpg image, select File, Export As. (Fig 38)

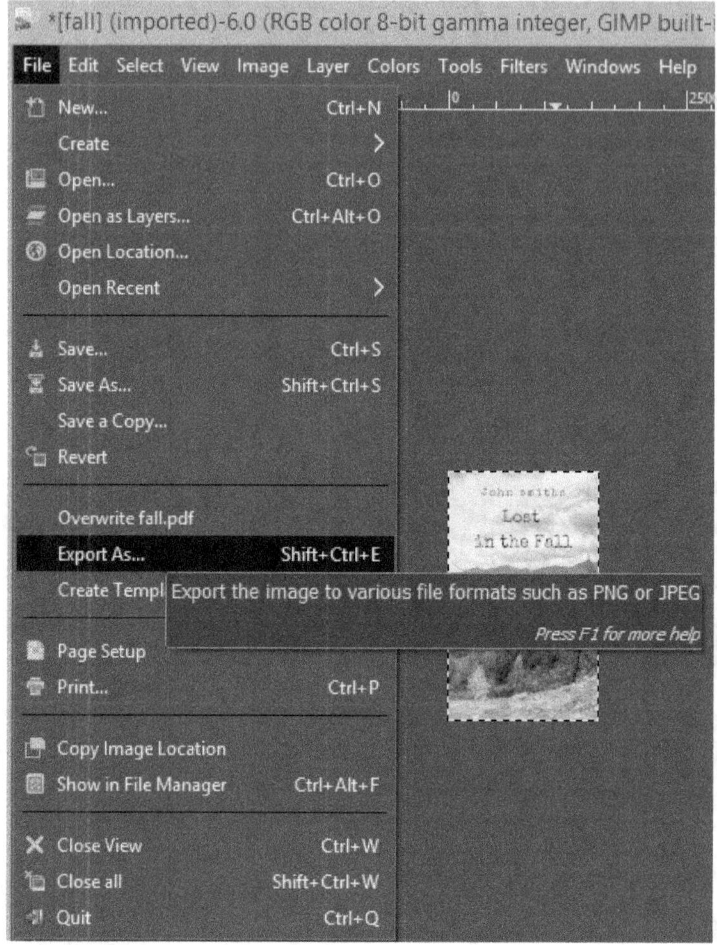

Figure 38. Export As.

A new window will appear. Enter the file name, select the JPEG format, and click the Export button. (Fig. 39)

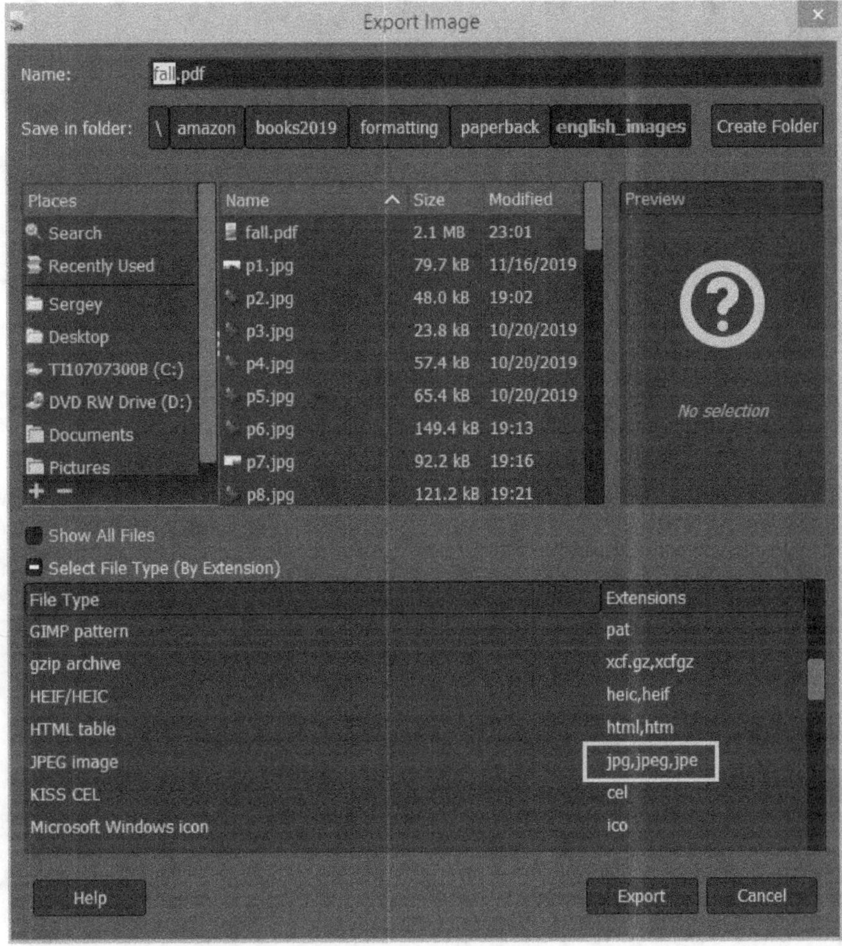

Figure 39. Export image.

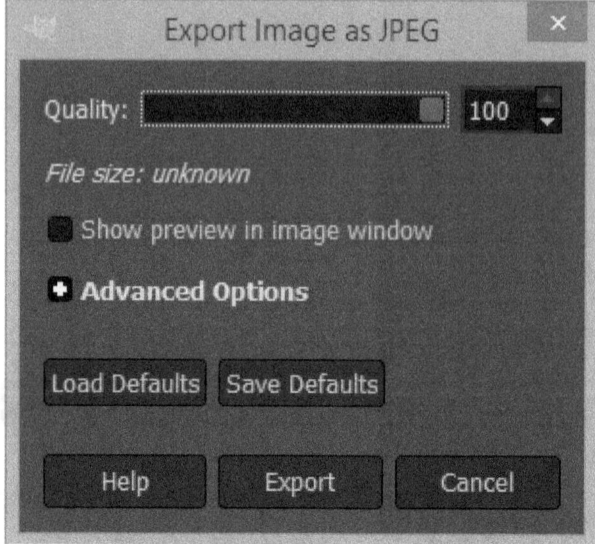

Figure 40. Export JPEG file.

In the next window, set quality to 100 and click the Export button. The cover is saved in JPEG format with a resolution of 300 dpi.

Find the saved cover. Put your mouse on it and press the right button. Select Properties from the menu.

On the Details tab, you can verify that the resolution is 300 dpi. (Fig. 41).

Figure 41. Resolution of the image 300 dpi.

4 How to Make a Three-Dimensional Cover for Advertising Your Book

When you publish a book, for its promotion, you will need to place on your website or a social media website, the cover of the book with a link to the web page on which readers can buy it. 3D covers look more attractive.
You can create a 3D cover using the designrr.io website. It has four plans: Standard, Pro, Premium and Business. You can see it here:
https://designrr.io/pricing/
To be able to create a 3D cover, you have to select at least the Pro plan. They have a 7 days free trial.

When you login to your account, select the MEDIA MANAGER from the main menu. (Fig. 42)

Figure 42. The Designrr.io website.

The Media Manager window is displayed. Click the Upload Image button and upload your cover. (Fig. 43)

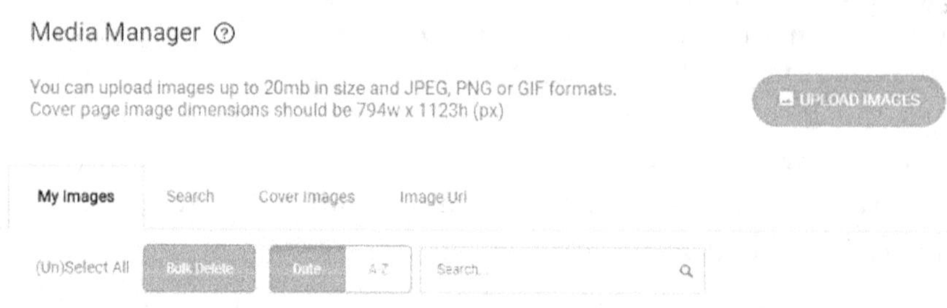

Figure 43. Upload image.

The image cover will be displayed on the Media Manager page. Hover your mouse over the image cover and the 3D icon will be visible. Click it.

(Fig.44).

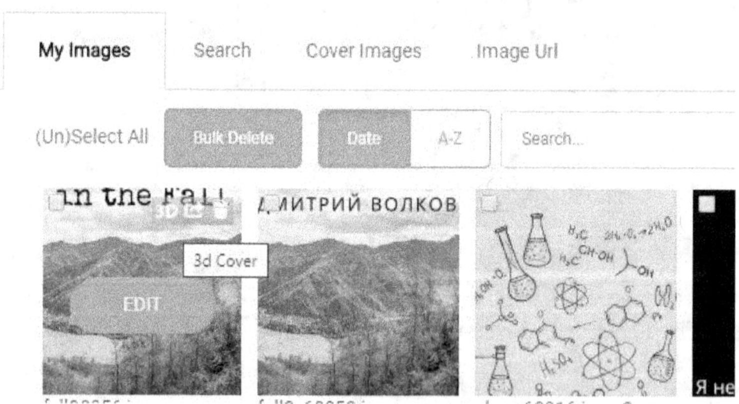

Figure 44. 3D cover icon

The Cover & Mockup Creator window is displayed. (Fig. 45)

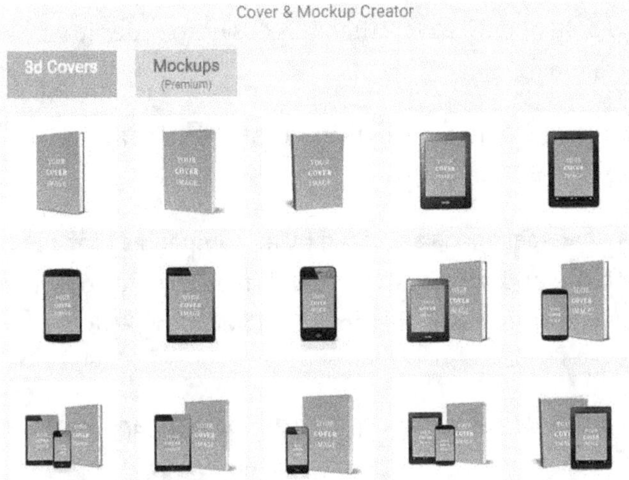

Figure 45. Different 3D book images.

Select any book composition and click it. The 3D composition will be displayed. (Fig. 46)

Figure 46. One of the selected 3D images.

There is another website where you can create a 3D cover: https://bookbrush.com.

If you need to make only one 3D cover, then it is easier to order it on the site http://fiverr.com.

5 How to Create an E-Book in Epub Format

The EPUB format is universal and is accepted by all companies that provide authors with the opportunity to self-publish electronic books. Therefore, it is very important to be able to create books in EPUB format.

To create a book in EPUB format, you can use free software applications such as Calibre and Sigil.
At the end of the book you will find detailed instructions for installing each application. These applications exist for both Windows PC and MAC. I used applications on my Windows PC.

You can download the Calibre application here: https://calibre-ebook.com/download_windows64

You can download the Sigil application here: https://www.techspot.com/downloads/5797-sigil.html

You can download the Adobe Digital Edition application here:

https://www.adobe.com/solutions/ebook/digital-editions/download.html.

The Adobe Digital Edition program is needed to check the finished book in EPUB, but more on that later.

You must also have Microsoft Word 2007 or later. Starting with this version, files have the docx extension.

The Calibre application allows you to convert docx format files to EPUB format.

Files from an earlier version of Microsoft Word have the doc extension and cannot be used in Calibre.

You wrote a book in Microsoft Word 2007 or later, the book has been edited and is ready for publication. In the process of working on the book, you made a lot of corrections, as a result your file contains many Microsoft Word codes that are not visible to you but can create problems when converting a Microsoft Word document to the EPUB format. You must create a new, clean Microsoft Word document. To do this, you should copy all the text from the Microsoft Word document and transfer it to Notepad or any other simple text editor that does not support text styles. To do that, in the Microsoft Word document, press Ctrl + A and the text is highlighted. Then press Ctrl + C and the text is copied to the clipboard. Then open Notepad and press the key combination Ctrl + V. All text is inserted into Notepad.

 In Notepad, press Ctrl + A, all text is highlighted. Then press Ctrl + C to copy the text to the clipboard. After that you open a new blank document in Microsoft Word and press Ctrl + V to paste text from Notepad back into the Microsoft Word document. In the Microsoft Word document, you should format your text again. (Fig. 47)

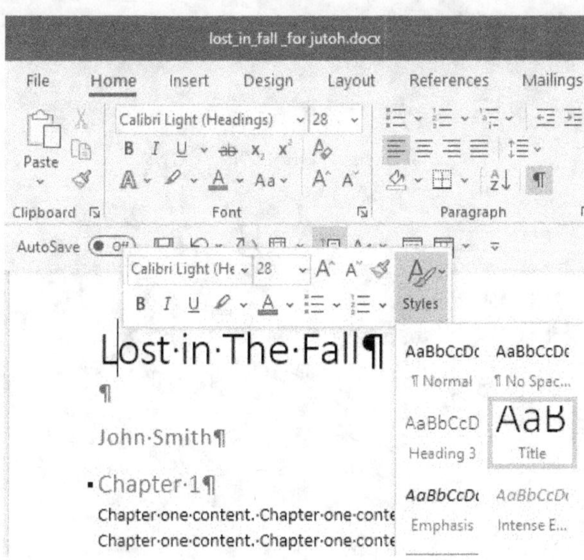

Figure 47. The title style.

Right-click the book title and select the Heading1 style as shown in Figure 47.

Right-click the author name and select the Subtitle style. (Fig. 48)

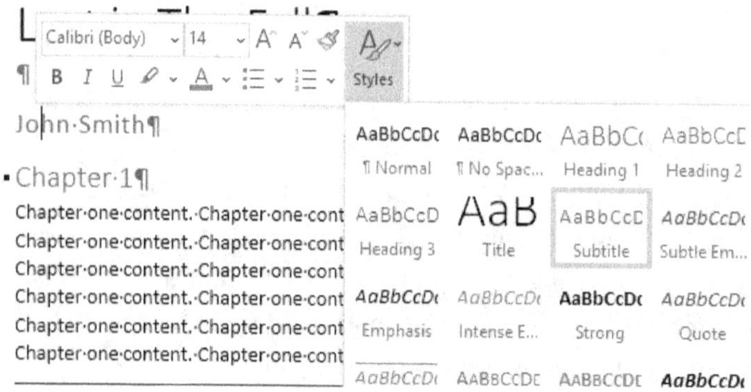

Figure 48. The author name style.

Right-click the title of the chapter and select the Heading 2 style. Repeat the procedure for each chapter title. (Fig. 49)

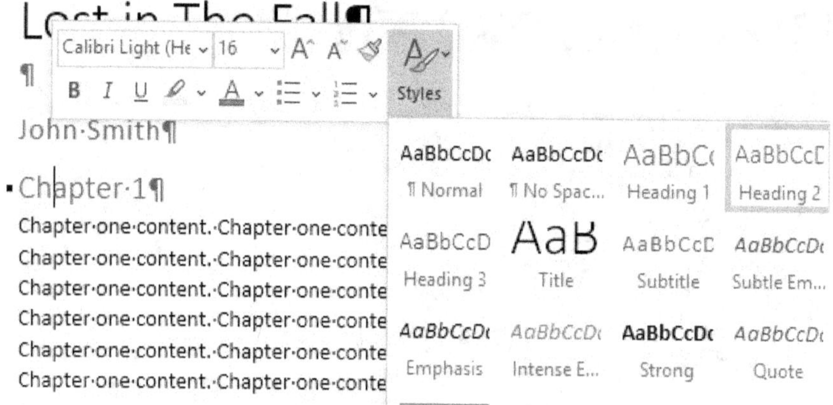

Figure 49. The chapter title style.

Right click on the chapter text and select Normal style. Figure 50.

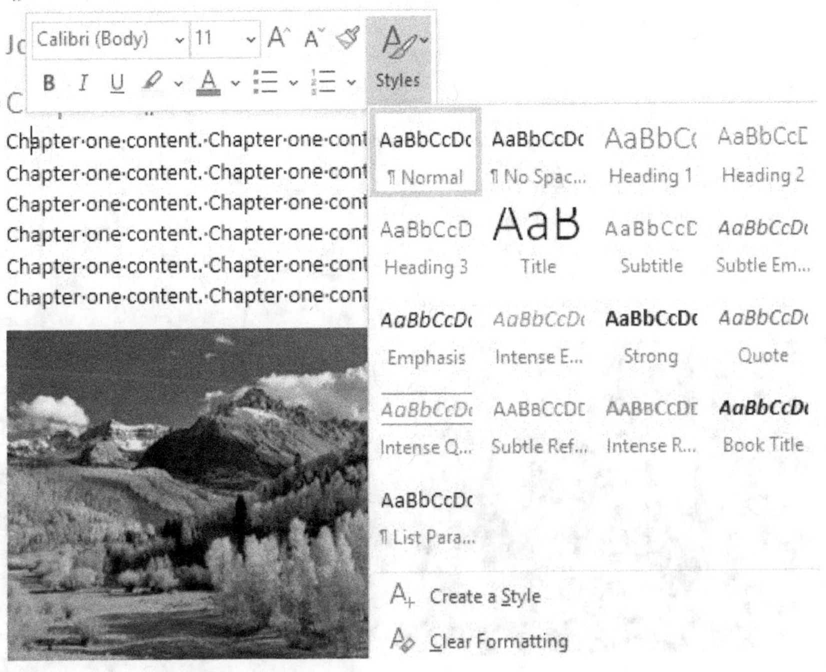

Figure 50. The main text style.

if you need to modify a style, select it, click the right mouse button and select Modify from the drop-down menu. (Fig. 51)

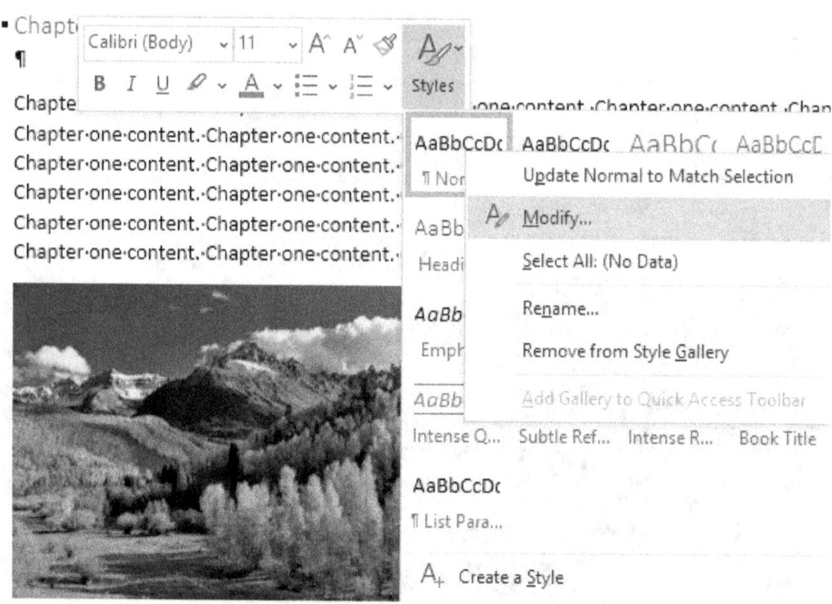

Figure 51. How to modify a style.

The Modify Style window is displayed. (Fig. 52)

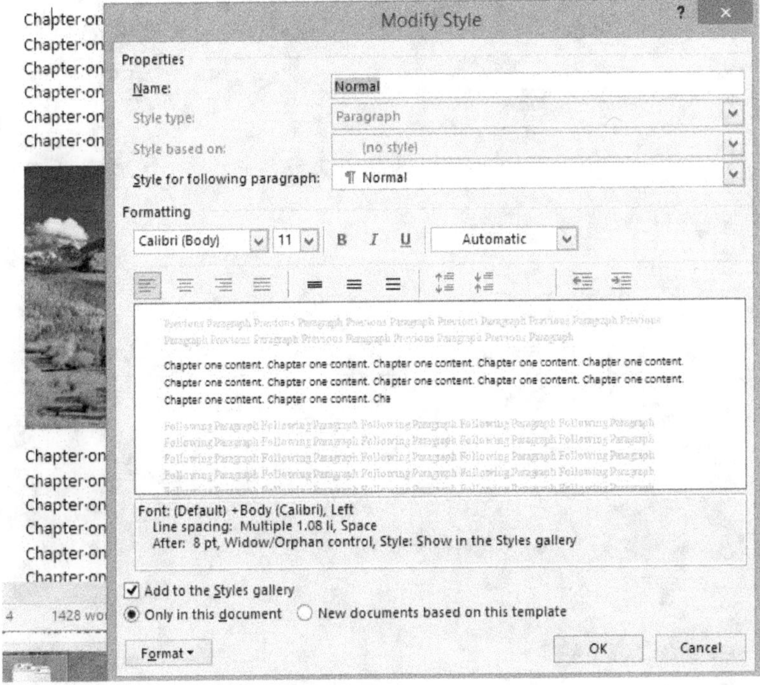

Figure 52. The modify style window.

Click the Format button and select Paragraph from the menu. (Fig. 53)

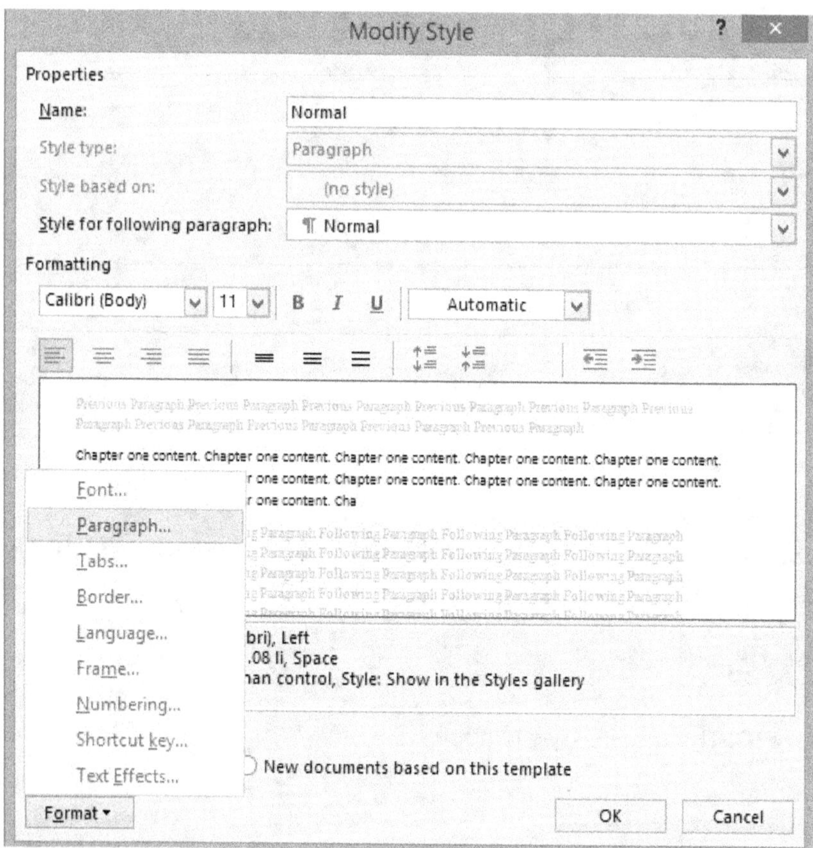

Figure 53. How to change the paragraph style.

A window will open for editing the paragraph. (Fig. 54)

In this window, set spacing to 0 (before and after) and select 'single' for the line spacing. Click the OK button on the Paragraph window and on the Modify Style window.

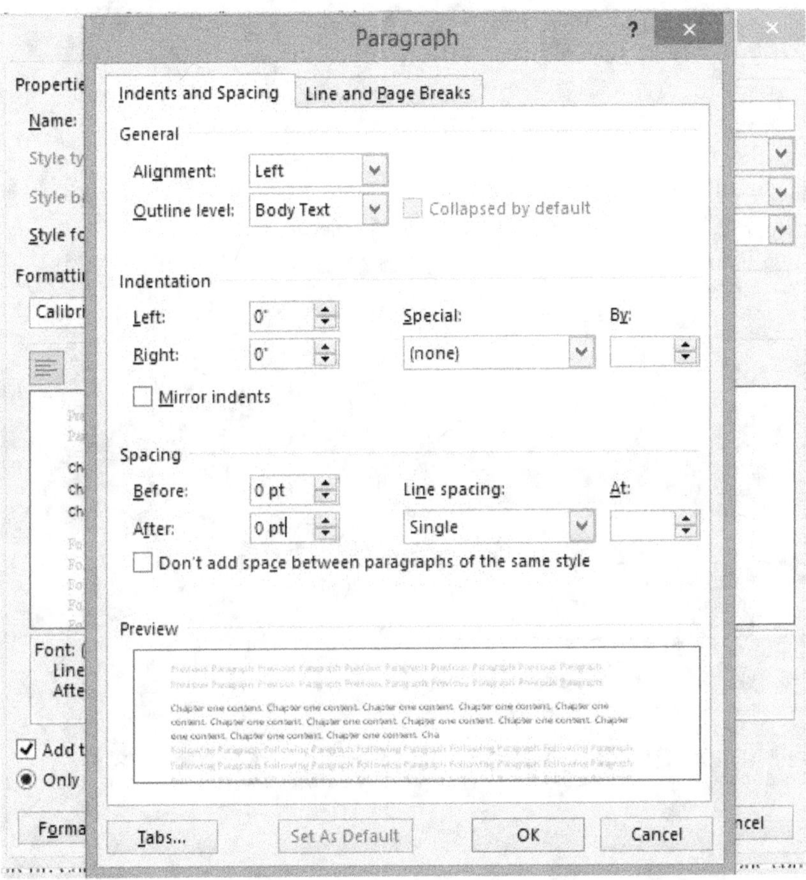

Figure 54. Modify spacing between the lines.

In the word document, select a chapter title and select the Heading 2 style from the styles. Right click on the Heading 2 style and select modify. On the modify Style window you can select a color for your chapter title different to than the black. (Fig. 55)

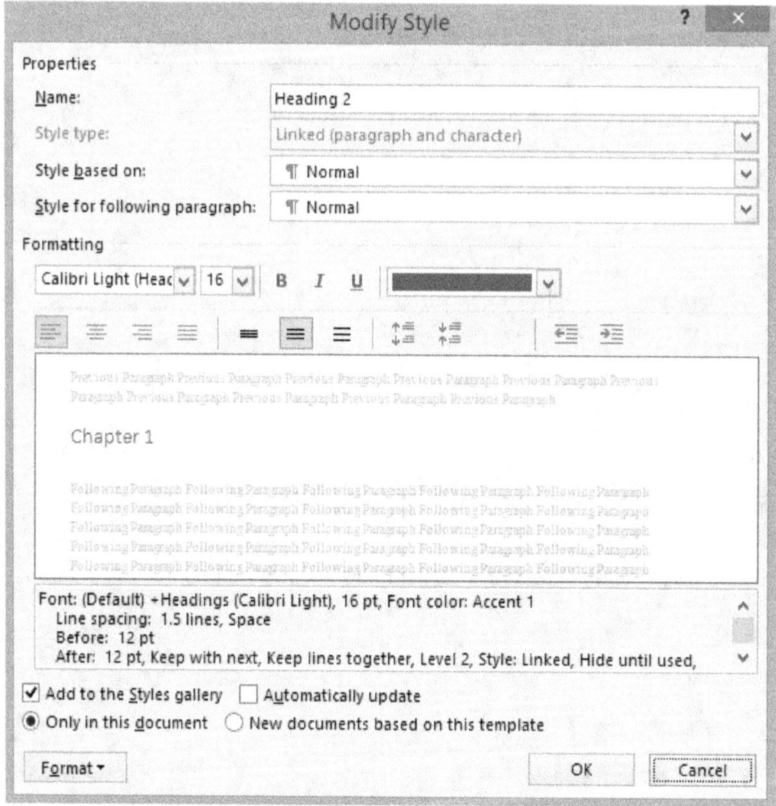

Figure 55. Formatting the chapter title.

Do not forget to save the word document after each modification.
Since the screen size is different for different devices, the e-book has no pages. Therefore, there is no table of contents with page numbers. In an e-book, a table of contents is like a website menu.
To make a table of contents, you just need to list all the chapter titles and put this list on a separate page after the title of the book and the name of

the author page. At the end of the book you can put a list of all your books and information about the author.

Links to websites where your books are sold are not recommended. For example, if you have a link to a book that is sold on Amazon, then Apple will not accept such a book, as Amazon and Apple are competitors.

It is better to have a link to a webpage on your website where you have a list of all your books with links to all websites where your books can be purchased. Also, it is useful to have at the end of your book a link to a reader magnet page where the readers can subscribe to your mailing list. When Your Word file is ready. Save it as a docx document.

5.1 Convert Docx Document To Epub Format

To convert a docx document to EPUB format, open the Calibre application. (Fig. 56).

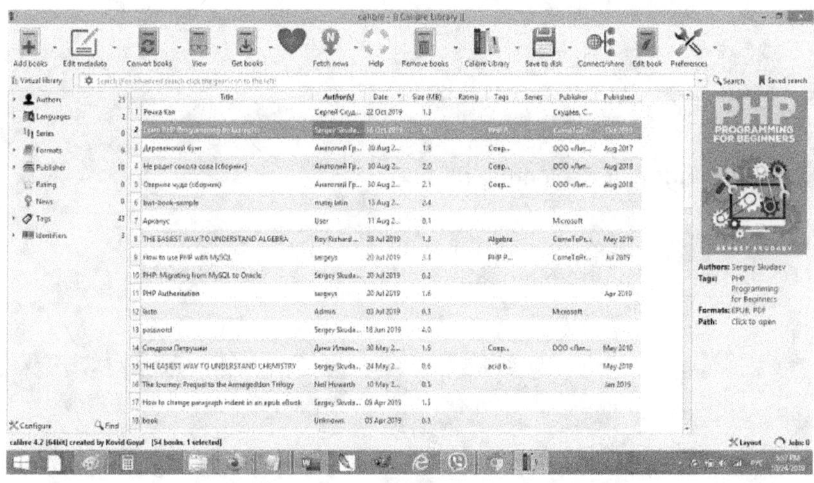

Figure 56 Calibre application

Click the **+** button and a window for selecting files is displayed.

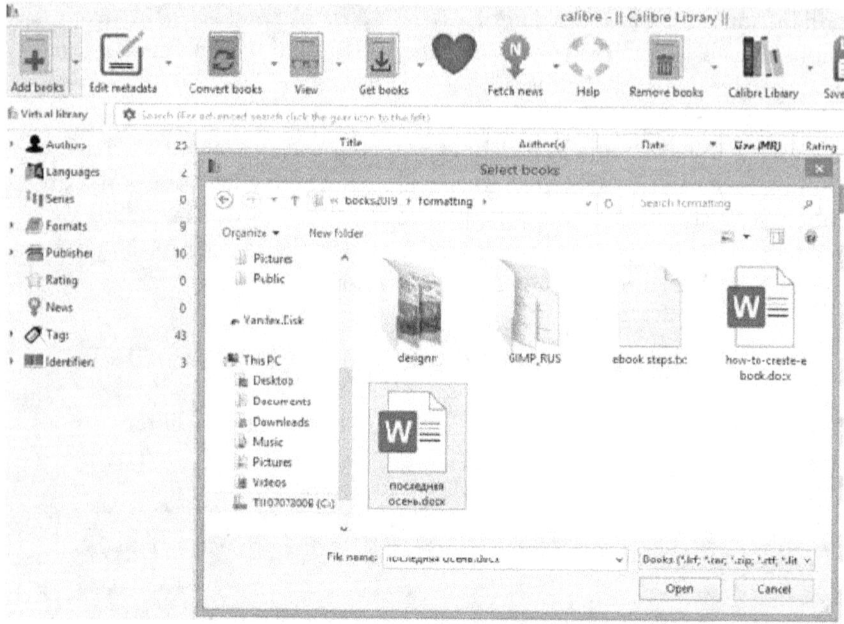

Figure 57. Window for selecting files.

Select the docx file with your book and click the Open button. The file will be added to Calibre. (Fig. 58)

Figure 58. The book in docx format has been added to Calibre.

To convert a book to a different format, click on the Convert books icon. A window will open for converting the book to EPUB format.

Click on the folder icon and select a cover. (Fig. 59).

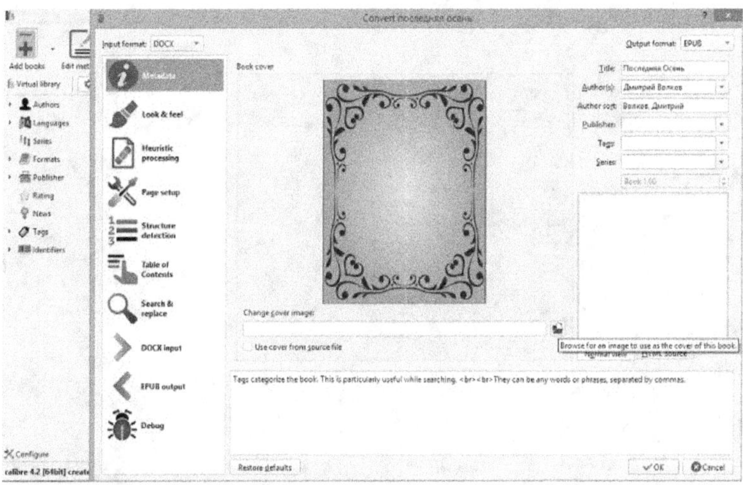

Figure 59. Conversion to EPUB. Adding a cover.

Enter your book metadata: a title, author name, publisher, etc. (Fig. 60)

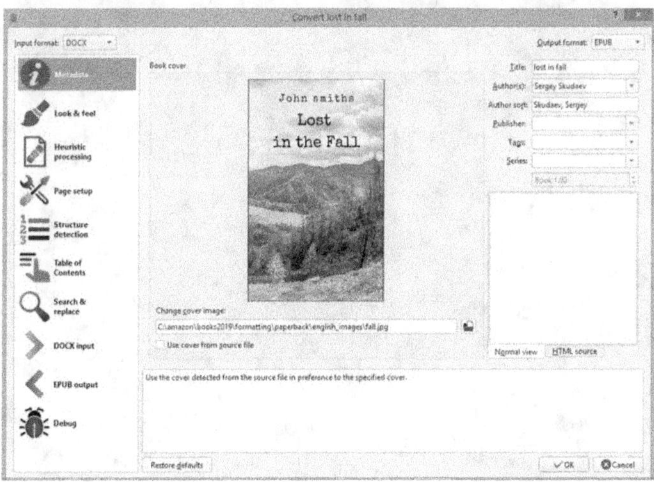

Figure 60. The cover is added.

Select the EPUB output option on the left panel. (Fig 60) Look at the option "Split files larger than 260 kb". Fig(61)

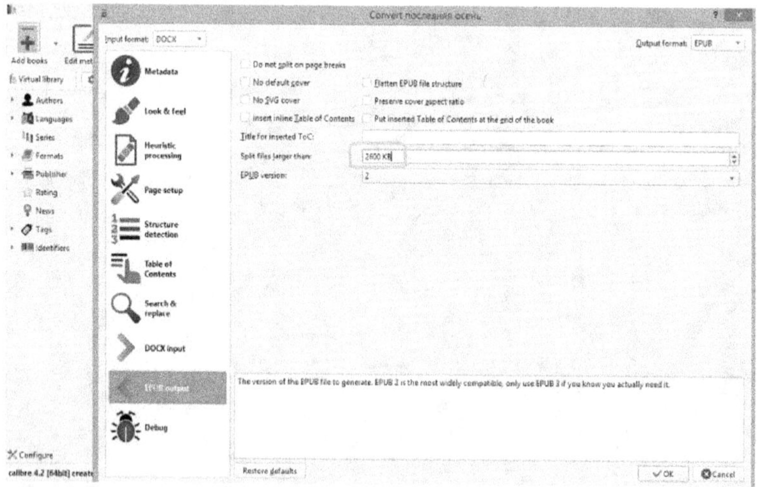

Figure 61. Split files larger than 260 kb

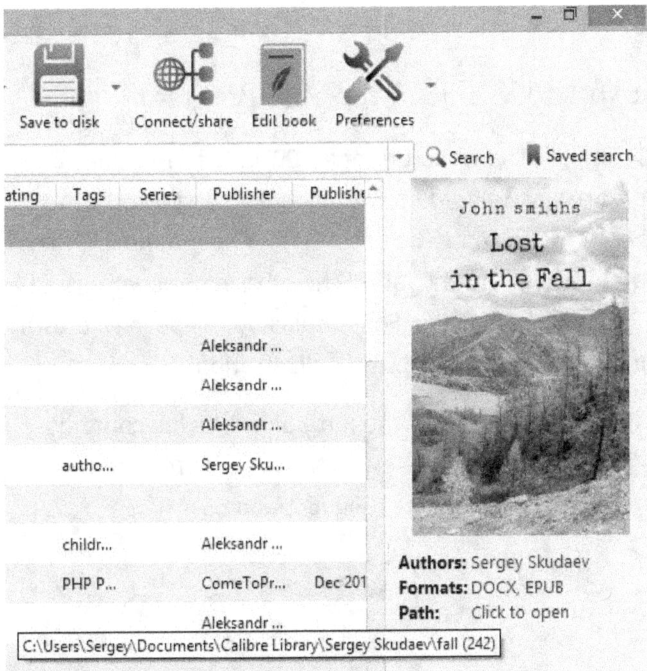

Figure 62. An EPUB file has been generated.

By default, if the text file is more than 260 kb, then it will be split into several html files. Leave it as it is.

An EPUB file is created. To find it, click the "Click to Open" link. (Fig. 62).

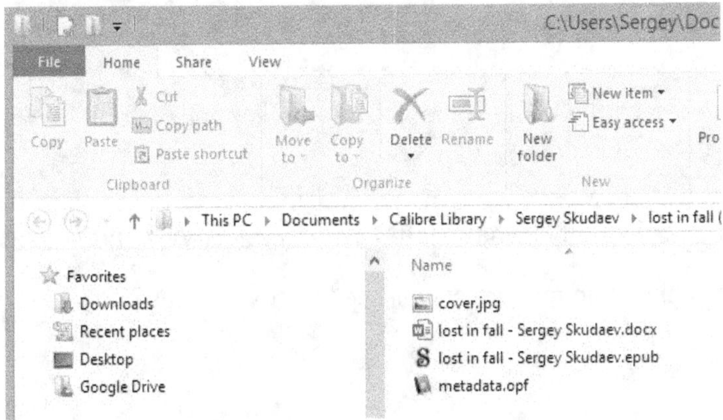

Figure 63. Files created in the process of converting a word document into EPUB format.

6. How to Edit an EPUB File in the Sigil Program

Open the EPUB file in Sigil. The structure of an EPUB file resembles a website. On the left are several folders with files. The first folder contains text files in HTML format. The second folder contains CSS files that contain styles, but more on that later. The next folder contains pictures: cover and book illustrations. For simplicity, I made in Microsoft Word a three-chapter demo book with three illustrations.

Select the index_split_000.html file in the left pane. This file contains the text of the book. Select View, Preview in the center of the main menu. You will see the text of the book. (Fig. 64, and 65).

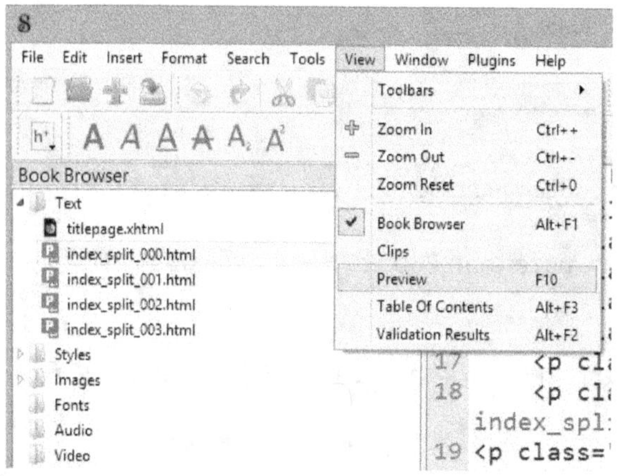

Figure 65. The text of the book. Table of contents.

Select the titlepage.xhtml file in the left pane and select View, Preview

in the center of the main menu. You will see the cover of the book.

(Fig. 66).

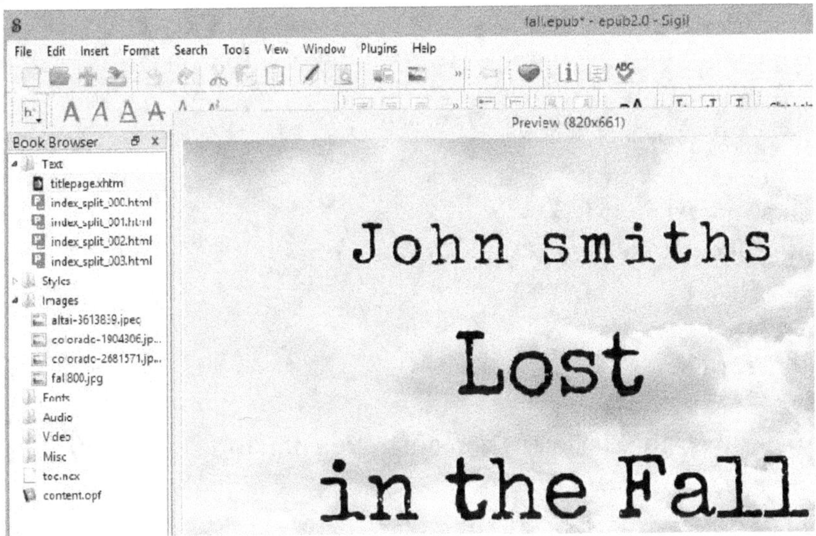

Figure 66. The structure of the EPUB file. The cover.

To edit the ebook manually, you have to know HTML and CSS.

But even if you don't know HTML, don't worry. You only need to know the minimum. HTML includes tags. For example, the <p> and </p> tags indicate the beginning and end of a paragraph. The <h1> and </h1> tags indicate the beginning and end of the main heading. The <h2> and </h2> tag is the beginning and end of a sub heading and so on. The <span> and </span> tags are used to style a part of the text within a paragraph. The <br /> tag means line break. It does not have an end tag. That's probably all you need to know about HTML.

To understand HTML and CSS, let's do some exercises. Type in the notepad the following HTML script for the simplest web page. (Fig. 67). The script of the web page begins with a statement of the type of the document. Then the language is declared, the head tag follows next. Between the <head> and </head> tags are the <title> and </title> tags. The main content of the page is located between the <body> and </body> tags. (Fig.67)

demo1.html

```
<!DOCTYPE html>
<html lang="en">
<head>
<meta charset="utf-8">
<title>Demo Web Page</title>
</head>
<body>
<h1>Dear Fiends!</h1>

<p>This web page is for the demonstration of HTML and CSS.</p>

</body>
</html>
```

Figure 67. The simplest webpage script.

Save the file as demo.html and open it in any browser. It is better to use Chrome or Firefox browsers.

You will see a large heading " Dear Fiends!" Because it is between the h1 tags.

The text, "This is a web page to demonstrate HTML and CSS." will be a normal fonts size because it is between the paragraph tags: <p> and </p>. (Fig. 68)

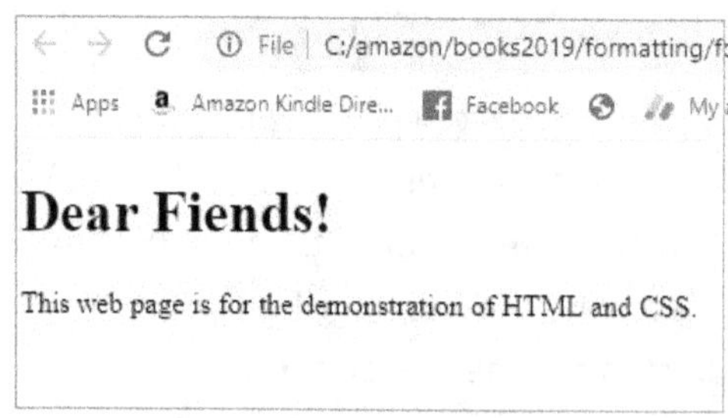

Figure 68. The simplest webpage.

Open your demo.html file in notepad and add a CSS class to change the color of the h1 header.

Please note that the CSS script should be placed between the <style> and </style> tags.

The <style> and </style> tags should be placed between the <head> and </head> tags.

The CSS class name must be preceded by a period. Curly brackets enclose class style properties. In our case, the color of the text. The class is assigned to the page header and the color of the header will be changed. (Fig. 69)

```
<!DOCTYPE html>
<html lang="en">
 <head>
 <meta charset="utf-8">
 <title>Demo Web Page 2</title>
 <style>

.blue-color {
color:#0000ff;
}

 </style>
 </head>
<body>
<h1 class="blue-color">Dear Fiends!</h1>

<p>This web page is for the demonstration of HTML and CSS.</p>

 </body>
 </html>
```

Figure 69. The CSS class "blue-color" has been added.

The header will be blue. (Fig. 70) . Open the file in the browser and you will see webpage changes.

Figure 70. The header color is blue: # 0000ff.

Open the demo.html file again in notepad and add two more classes: abc and xyz.

You can use any combination of letters as the class name. In the abc class, we set the text to yellow and the background to blue. In the xyz class, we assign a blue color to the text and a yellow color to the background. We assign the xyz class to the paragraph and assign the abc class to a part of the text between the <span> and </span> tags. In Figure 71 two CSS classes "abc" and "xyz" are added. (Fig. 71)

demo3.html

```
<!DOCTYPE html>
<html lang="en">
<head>
<meta charset="utf-8">
<title>Demo Web Page 3</title>
<style>
.blue-color {
color:#0000ff;
}
 .abc {
color: yellow;
background-color: blue;
}
 .xyz {
color: blue;
```

```
background-color: yellow;
}
</style>
</head>
<body>
<h1 class="blue-color">Dear Fiends!</h1>
 <p class="xyz">This web page is for the demonstration of <span class="abc">HTML и CSS</span></p></body></html>
```

Figure 71. HTML page 3.

Open the file in the browser and you will see the webpage changes. (Fig. 72)

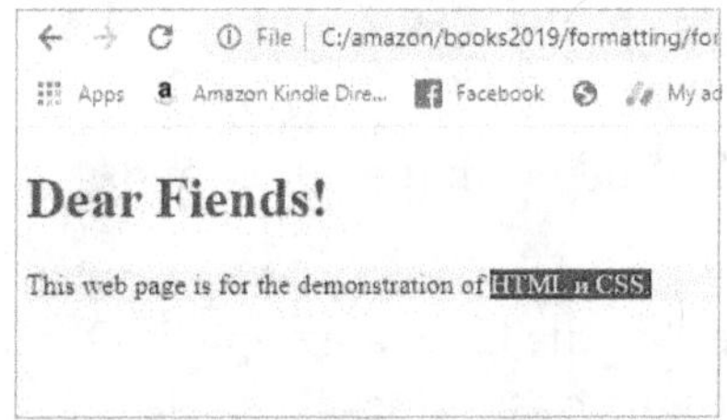

Figure 72. The background and text color of the paragraph and parts of the text have changed according to CSS classes.

The style of various parts of the text can be set using classes.
Now let's go back to our book. Open your EPUB file in the Sigil application.
In Figure 73, you will see the HTML script of the book page. (Fig. 73)

```
 7        <title>Lost in The Fall</title>
 8        <meta http-equiv="Content-Type" conter
html; charset=utf-8"/>
 9    <link href="../Styles/stylesheet.css"
rel="stylesheet" type="text/css"/>
10 <link href="../Styles/page_styles.css"
rel="stylesheet" type="text/css"/>
11 </head>
12    <body class="calibre">
13      <p class="block_">Lost in The Fall</p>
14      <p class="block_1"> </p>
```

Figure 73. HTML page code.

Copy the title of the book "Lost in The Fall" between the <title> and </title> tags.

In the HTML script, in Figure 73, you see that the first paragraph has the class "block_". The second paragraph has the class "block_1". A class can be named as you like. What "class" means can be found in the stylesheet.css file.

CSS stays for Cascading Style Sheets. CSS describes how a web page element should be displayed in the browser. Place the mouse on the stylesheet.css file and see what is inside. (Fig. 74)

```
 1 .block_ {
 2     color: black;
 3     display: block;
 4     font-family: sans-serif;
 5     font-size: 2em;
 6     letter-spacing: -0.5pt;
 7     line-height: 1.2;
 8     margin: 0;
 9     padding: 0
10     }
```

Figure 74. CSS - Cascading style sheets.

Let's look at what the "block_" class consists of. The class name in the

CSS file must be preceded by a period.

After the class name, the class properties are placed in curly brackets. After the property name a colon must be placed. The value of the property goes after the colon and a semicolon is closing the code line.

For example, display: block;

display: block; - means that the element to which the class is assigned will begin with a new line and the next web page element will also begin with a new line.

By default, a paragraph is a block. It always starts on a new line.

Font-family: "Calibri Light", san-serif; - determines which font will be used for the text.

All fonts are divided into two types: serif and san-serif.

Popular sans-serif fonts are Helvetica and Arial. Popular serif fonts: Times Roman, Courier, and Palatino.

Sans-serif fonts consist of simple lines, while serif fonts use small decorative strokes that makes the text easier to read. (Fig. 75).

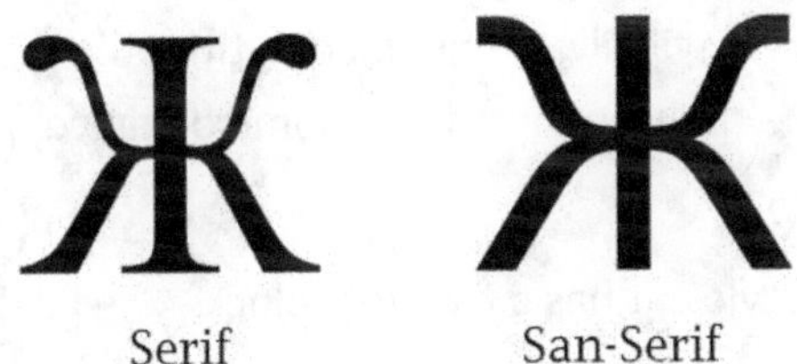

Figure 75.An example of serif and san-serif fonts.
Serif fonts are usually used for the body of the book, and san-serif fonts are usually used for headings. For a book, it's better not to use more than two fonts families. Which fonts to choose is not so important because when the book is read on various devices, the devices can replace your fonts with their own. It is better, however, to use popular fonts such as Times New Roman for serif and Arial for san- serif.

The following property is "font-size: 2em;" – this means that the size of the letters will be 2em. What is an em unit?
Em is a relative unit of measure. 1 em is equal to the height of the lowercase letter x.
2em - means that the text will be twice as large as the main text.
Letter-spacing: - 0.5pt; - means the distance between the letters. A negative value means that the text will be compressed. A positive value greater than 1 means that the letters will be spaced further apart.
Line-height: 1.2; - determines the height of the text line.
What does Padding mean? In CSS, the padding property sets the value of the padding of an element from the edge of a block frame. For our purposes, text padding will always be 0. This property can be ignored. (Fig. 76)

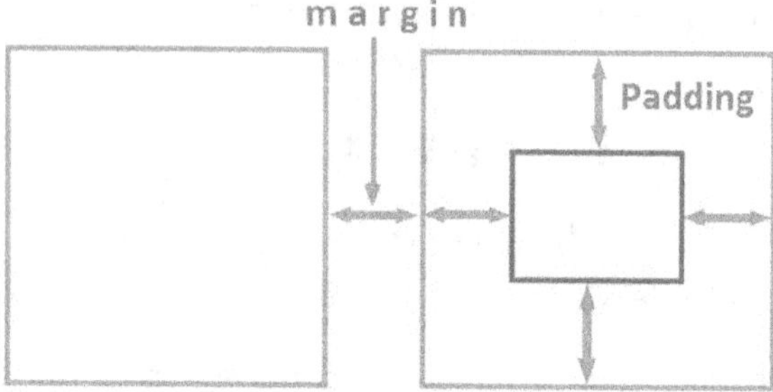

Figure 76. Margin and padding

Margin: 0 - sets the margin of the block from the neighboring block. For a paragraph in an e-book, the margin will always be 0. For a title, the margin can be greater than 0, since the title must be at some distance from the main text.

Let's investigate the chapter title styles. It has a class of "block_4". (Fig.77)

```
titlepage.xhtml    index_split_000.html    stylesheet.css    index_split_001.html
13 <h2 class="block_4"><a id="ch1">Chapter 1
   a></h2>
14 <p class="block_1"> </p>
15 <p class="block_2">
```

Figure 77. HTML code for the header <h2> of the first chapter. Class = "block_4".

Select the stylesheet.css file and see the definition of the "block_4" class. (Fig. 78)

```
titlepage.xhtml      index_split_000.html      stylesheet.css      index_split_001

35  .block_4 {
36      display: block;
37      font-family: sans-serif;
38      font-size: 1.29167em;
39      font-weight: normal;
40      line-height: 1.2;
41      page-break-after: avoid;
42      page-break-inside: avoid;
43      margin: 2pt 0 0;
44      padding: 0
45      }
```

Figure 78. Defining the class "block_4" in the stylesheet.css file.

Pay attention to such properties as page-break-after: avoid;
page-break-inside: avoid;
It means avoiding a page break after the heading and inside the heading. It is important to avoid having a title of a chapter on one page, and the text of the chapter on the next page.
If you need to force a page break after the end of the chapter, you can insert:
page-break-after: always;
in the class assigned to the last paragraph of the chapter. See Figures 79 and 80.

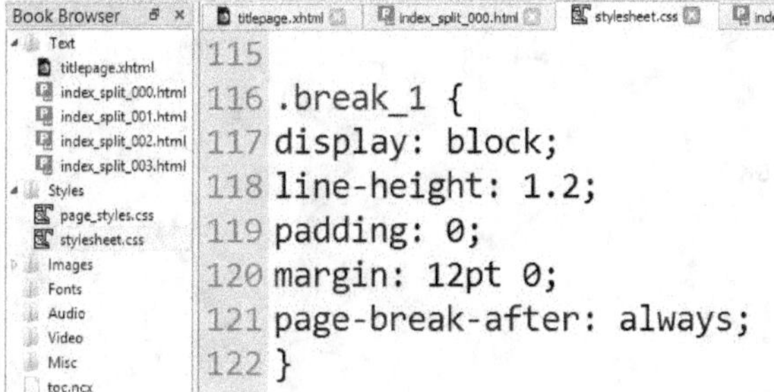

```
Book Browser                titlepage.xhtml      index_split_000.html      stylesheet.css      inde
Text
  titlepage.xhtml          115
  index_split_000.html
  index_split_001.html     116  .break_1 {
  index_split_002.html     117  display: block;
  index_split_003.html
Styles                     118  line-height: 1.2;
  page_styles.css          119  padding: 0;
  stylesheet.css           120  margin: 12pt 0;
Images                     121  page-break-after: always;
Fonts
Audio                      122  }
Video
Misc
toc.ncx
```

Figure 79. Break class definition.

```
<p class="block_1">
<a href="../Text/index_split_003.html#ch4">
About the author</a></p>
   <p class="break_1"> </p>
```

Figure 80. A paragraph with the class that forces the page break.

If you want to change the font size of the header, you can do this in the block_4 class. For example, change font-size to 1.4em or 1.2em. Or you can change the color of the title text. Type in google "html color picker" and open the page "HTML Color Picker - W3Schools". (Fig. 81).

Colors are encoded using hexadecimal digits. Example hexadecimal digits: 0123456789ABCDEF.

For example, the code for red is #ff0000, for green #00ff00, for blue #0000ff, and so on. To see the color of the code, copy the color code from the stylesheet.css file into the window of the W3Schools website and click OK. A set of colors appears on the right that are lighter and darker than your color. Select a new color, copy its code and paste it into "block_4". See Figure 78.

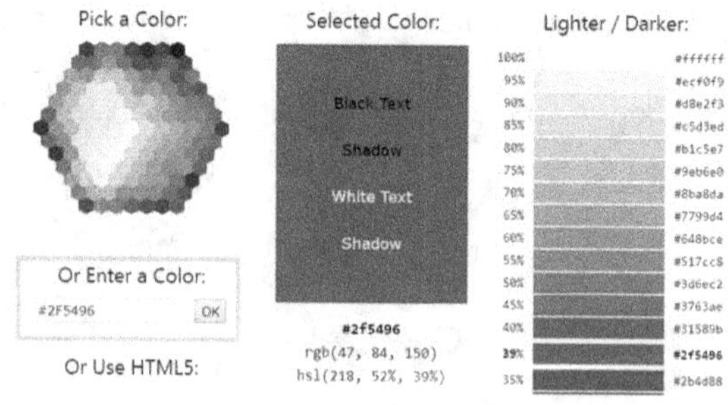

Figure 81. HTML Color Picker

6.1 How to Add Illustrations to the Text of the Book

For e-book illustrations, the size of photos should be 700 pixels wide and no more than 800-900 pixels in height. Otherwise, the image may not fit on the screen.

It is best to change the size and resolution of photos using Photoshop, as this does not spoil the image quality. Photoshop is an expensive, but the old version of Photoshop can be downloaded for free here:

https://www.techspot.com/downloads/3689-adobe-photoshop-cs2.html

The old version is quite sufficient for our purposes. (Fig. 82)

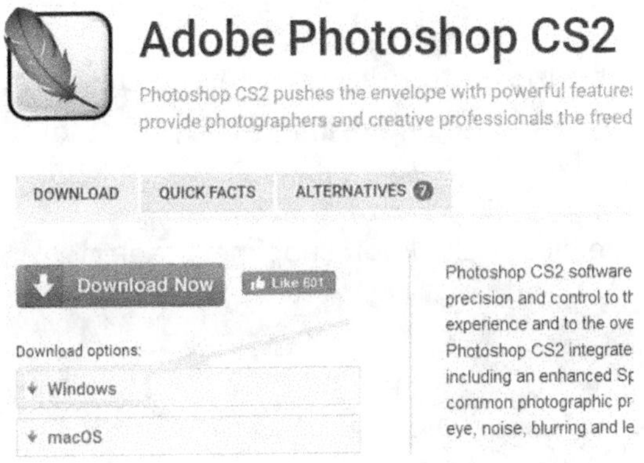

Figure 82. Download photoshop CS2.

When you are installing a free program, be careful not to install anything else that you do not need. Freeware often offers to install additional software.
In the process of writing this book, I used Photoshop to resize pictures and change their resolution. I will show you how to do this using, as an example, the following picture:

Figure 83. The original image is 2285 x 3107 pixels with a resolution of 72 DPI.

To make it smaller: 1600 x 2400 pixels with a resolution of 300 DIP open the image in Photoshop. Place the mouse on the image file, press the right button of the mouse and select - open with Adobe Photoshop CS2.

To change the resolution of the file, on the Photoshop menu, select Image, Image Size. (Fig. 84)

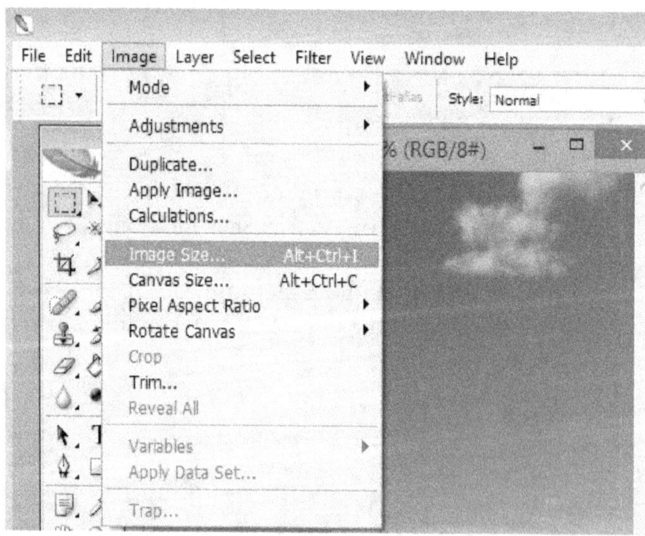

Figure 84. Image Size.

The image size window is displayed with the image dimension and resolution. (Fig.85)

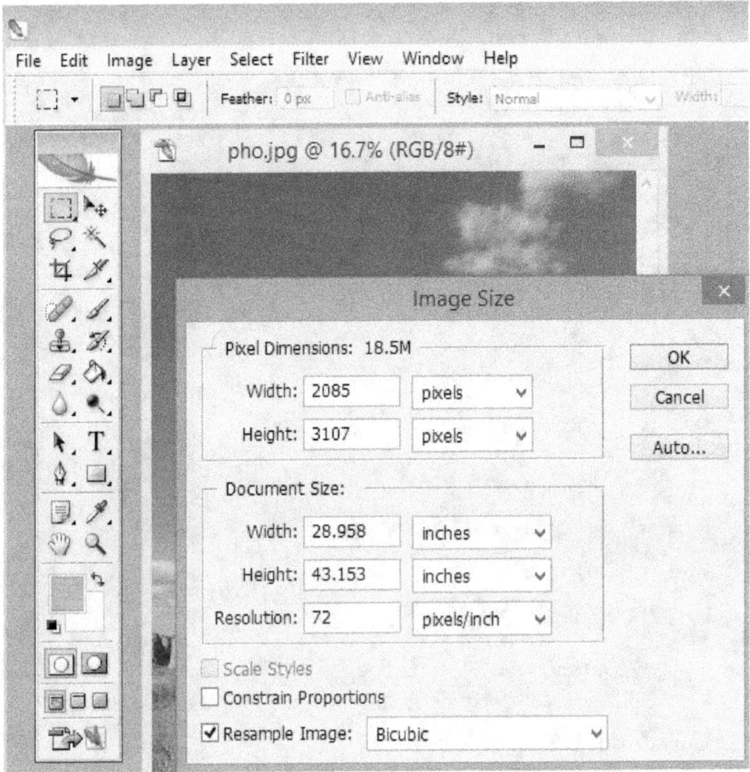

Figure 85. Changing the resolution of the image from 72 to 300.

Change the resolution of the image to 300. The width and height of the image is increased. (Fig. 86)

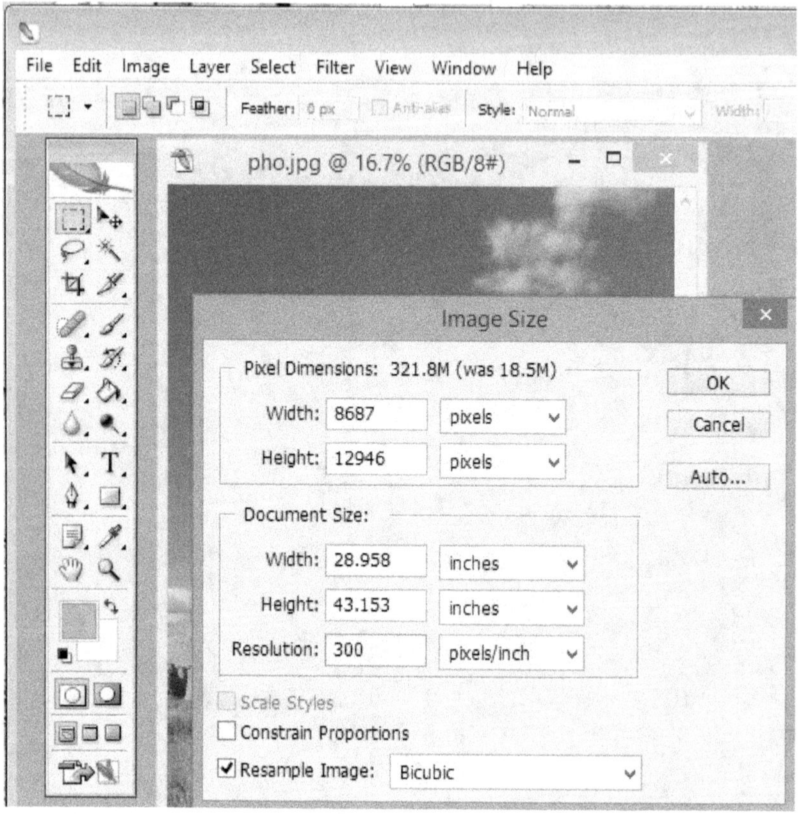

Figure 86. New resolution 300 DIP.

Change the size of the image back to the original: 2285 x 3107 pixels and save the picture. (Fig. 87)

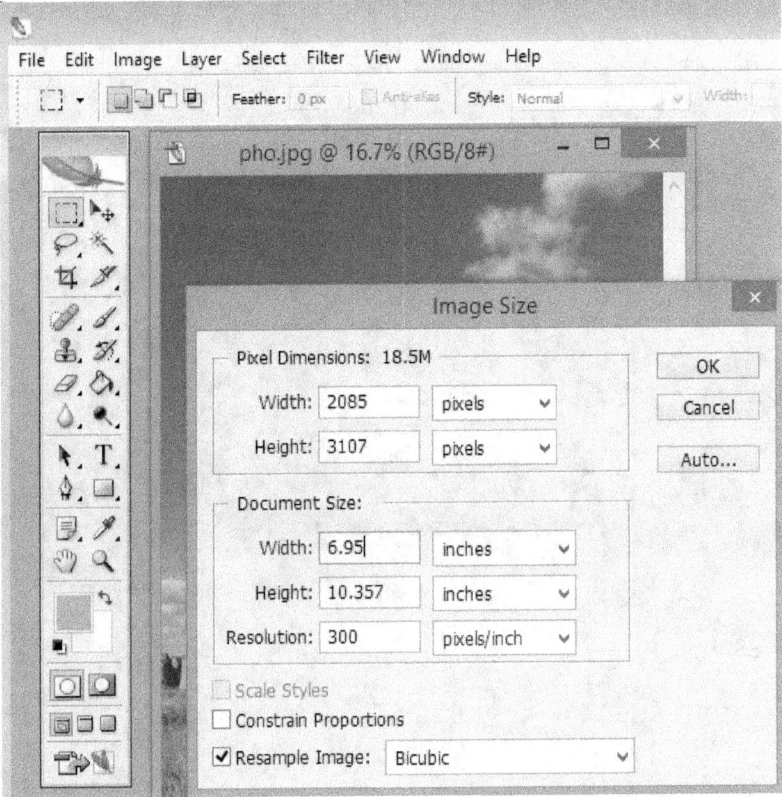

Figure 87. The size of the image is changed back to 2085 x 3107 pixels.

Now you have to save the image. On the main menu select File, Save As. (Fig.88)

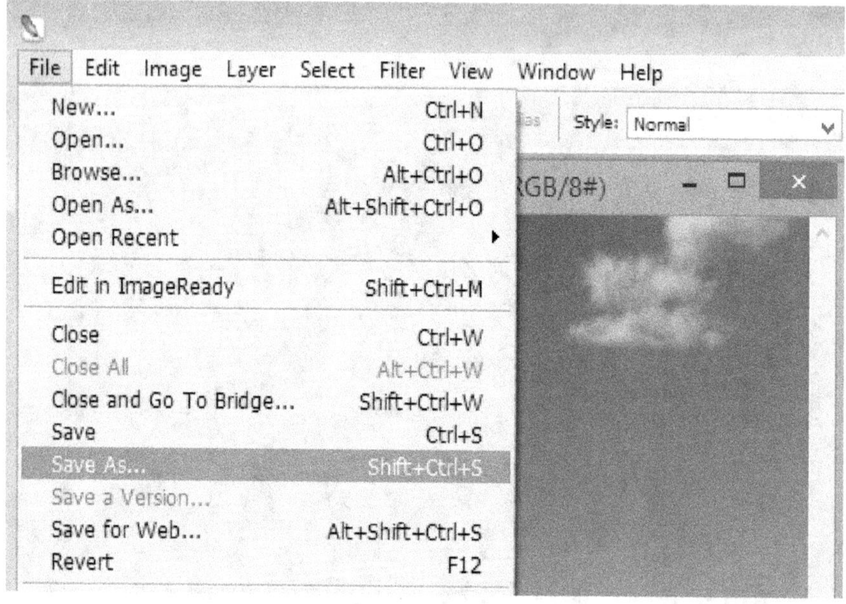

Figure 88. Save As.

The Save window will be displayed. (Fig. 89)

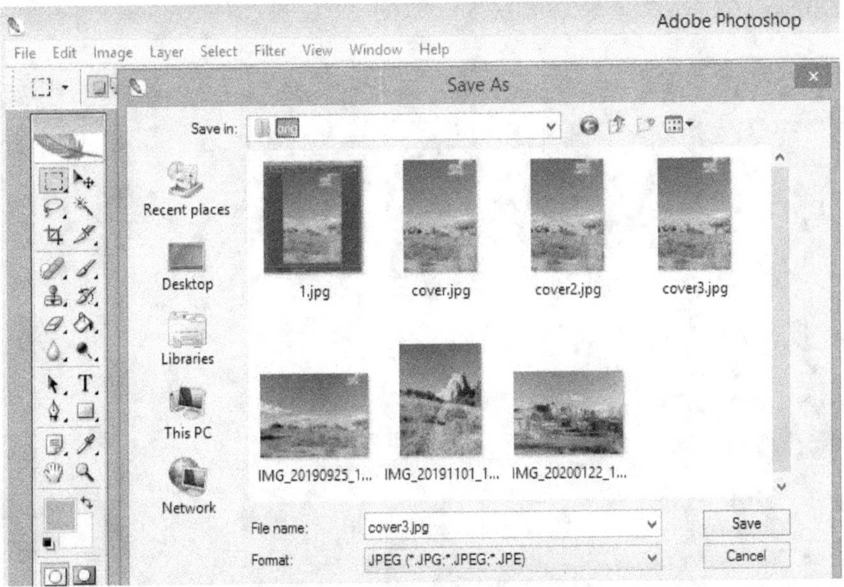

Figure 89. Save the image to a folder.

Select a folder where you want to save the image and click the Save button.

The quality option window will be displayed. (Fig. 90)

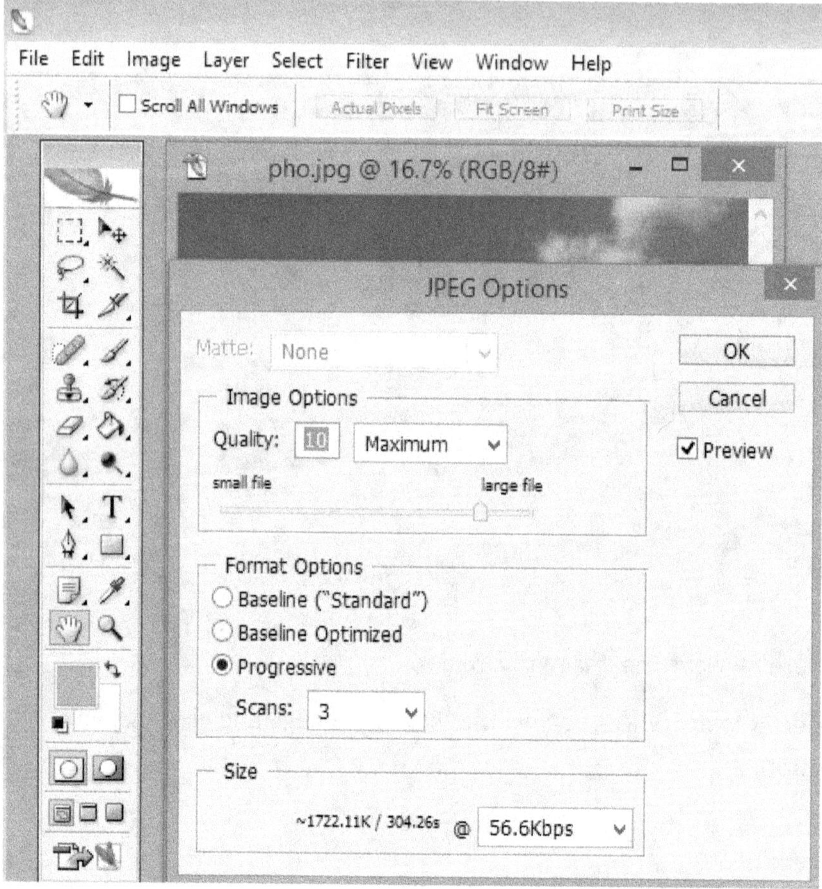

Figure 90. Select the maximum quality.

Select the maximum quality and click the OK button. The image will be saved. (Fig. 91)

Figure 91. Saved image with the new resolution 300 DIP. (2285 x 3107 pixels)

In the next window, set the width of the image to 1600 pixels. Height is set automatically.

If you do not want the aspect ratio of the image to be saved automatically, then you must remove the mark from the Constrain Proportion flag. Then you can set your width and height, thereby changing the proportions of the picture. But in most cases this is not necessary. (Fig. 92)

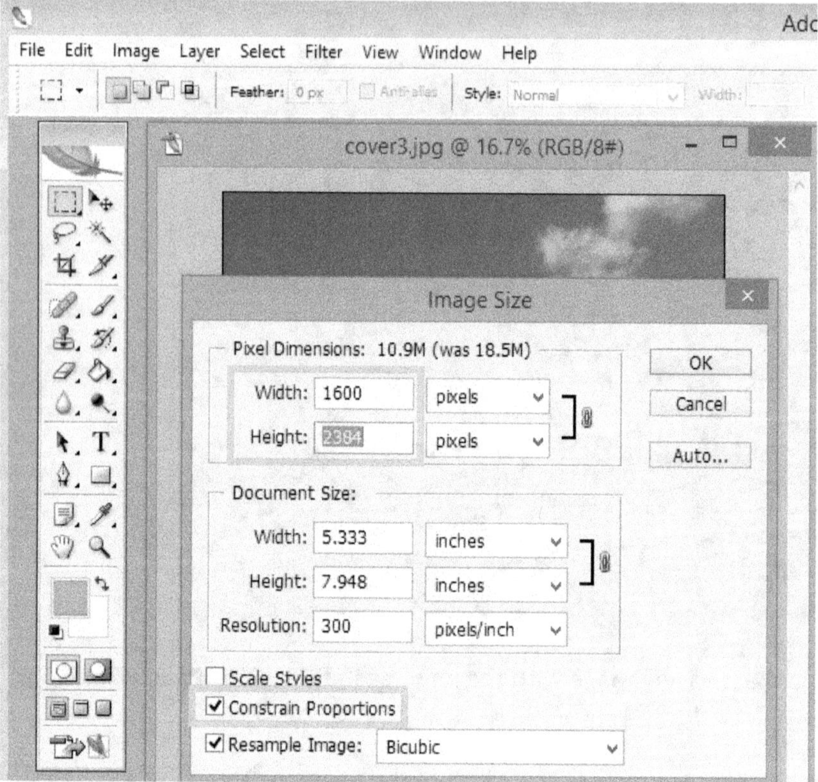

Figure 92. Resizing the image.

After you set the new image size, click the OK button. The image will be resized. To save the image select Save As from the File menu. (Fig. 93)

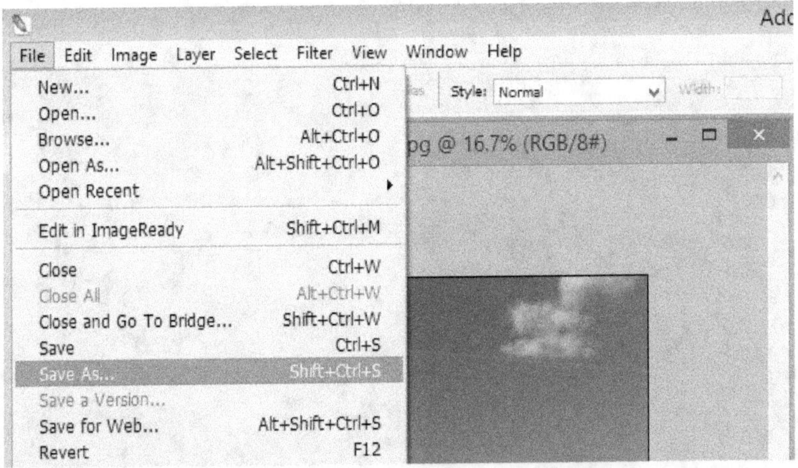

Figure 93. Saving the resized image.

The quality option window will be displayed. Select the maximum quality and click OK. (Fig.94)

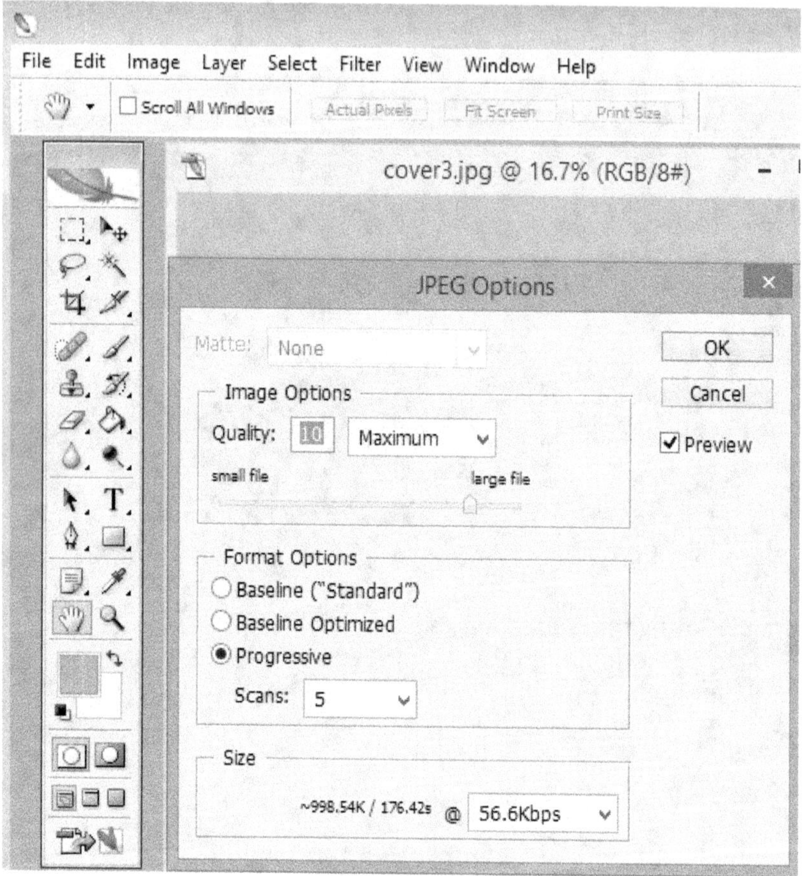

Figure 94. Selecting the quality of the image..

The resized image will be saved. (Fig. 95)

Figure 95. The resized image of 1600 x 2400 pixels.

To insert an image to the EPUB file, place mouse cursor on the page location where you want the image to be inserted and click the image icon on the main menu. See Figure 96.

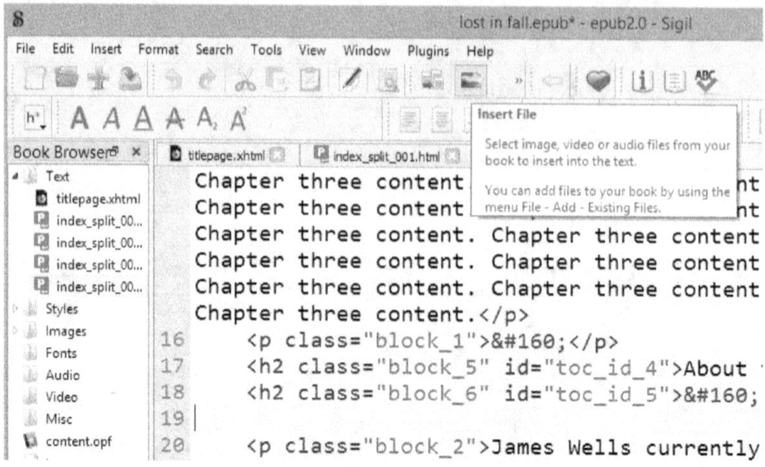

Figure 96. How to insert an image to the book.

A window for selecting an image will be opened. Click the Other Files button. (Fig. 97).

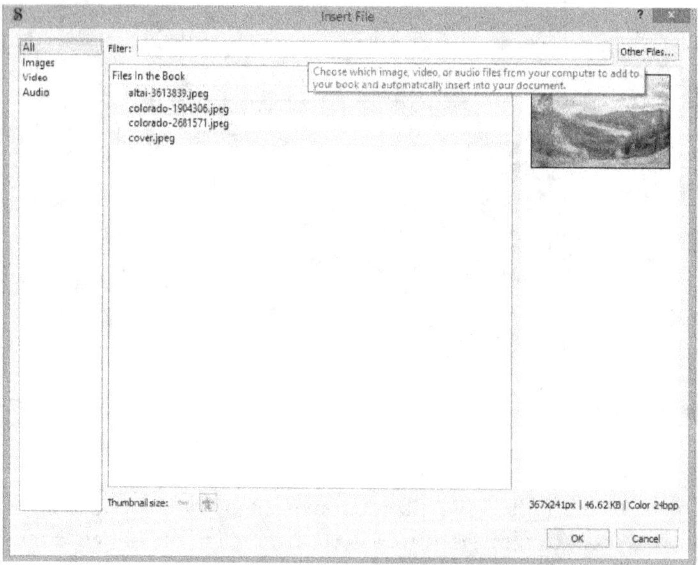

Figure 97. How to add an image to the book.

Find a suitable image in jpg format. Select the image and click the Open button. The image is inserted in the book. (Fig. 98)

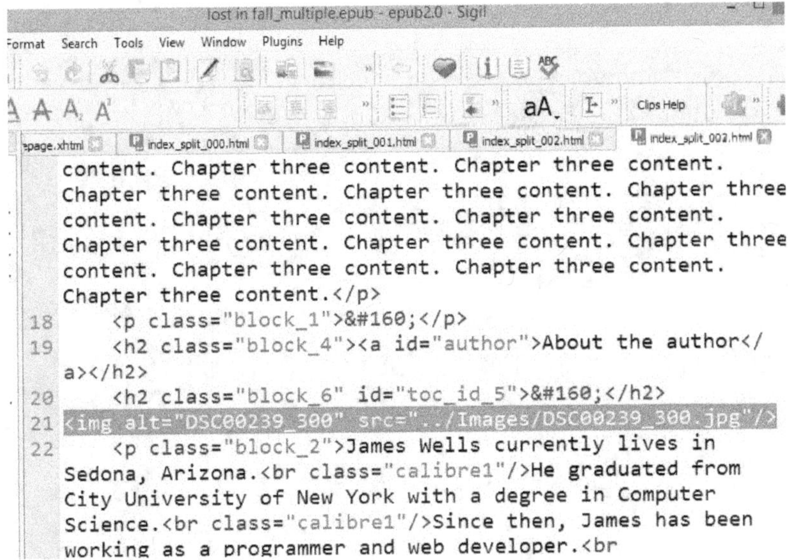

Figure 98. HTML code to display the inserted image is created automatically.

Select View, Preview from the main menu and display the page. The image is inserted in the book. (Fig. 99).

Figure 99. The image is inserted.

If you don't like a photograph and want to delete it, highlight the code with the image and press the Delete key on the keyboard. (Fig. 100).

```
index_split_000.html    stylesheet.css    index_split_001.html    index_split_002.html    index
16      <p class="block_1"> </p>
17 <img alt="me7" src="../Images/me7.jpg"/>
18      <p class="block_1"> </p>
19      <h2 class="block_4">
20 <a id="ch4">About the author</a></h2>
21      <h2 class="block_5"> </h2>
```

Figure 100. How to remove the image code.

After deleting the image code, delete the image file from the images folder. Right-click on the file and select the Delete option from the menu. (Fig. 101).

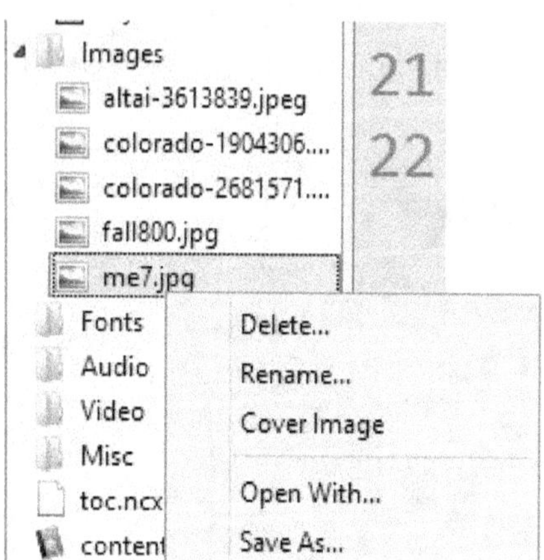

Figure 101. Deleting an image file.

In the window that opens, click the Delete Marked Files button. (Fig. 102)

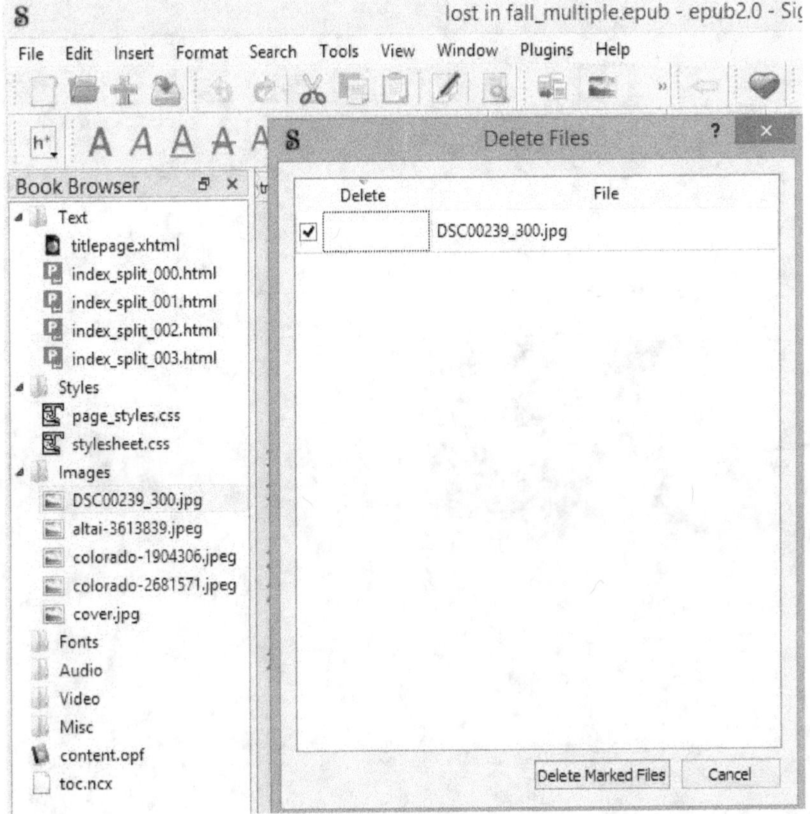

Figure 102. Deleting an image file.

Click the button in the yellow square and select another image.
(Fig 103).

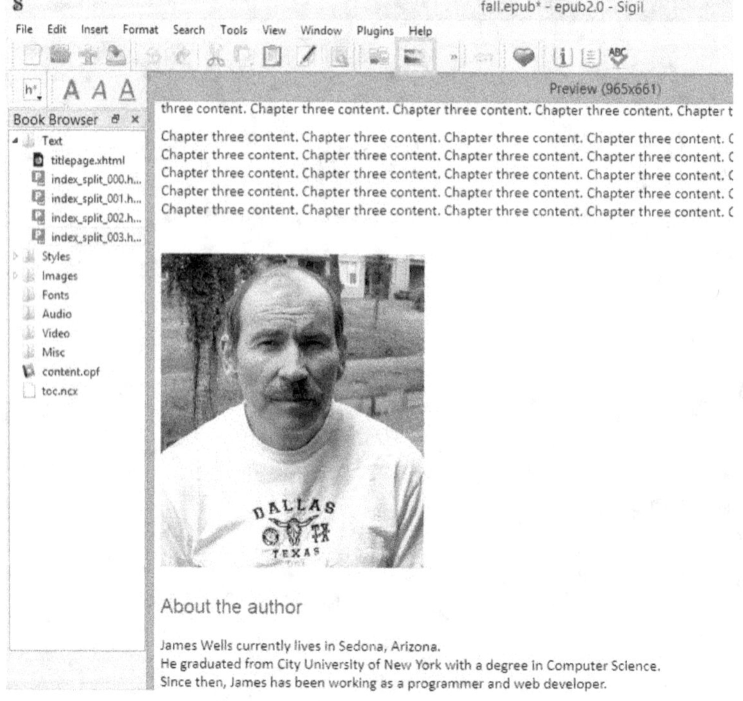

Figure 103. A new image is inserted into the book.

Do not forget to save the file after each change, to not lose what you have
done in case of a power outage.

To save the file, click the button in the yellow square or select: File , Save. (Fig. 104).

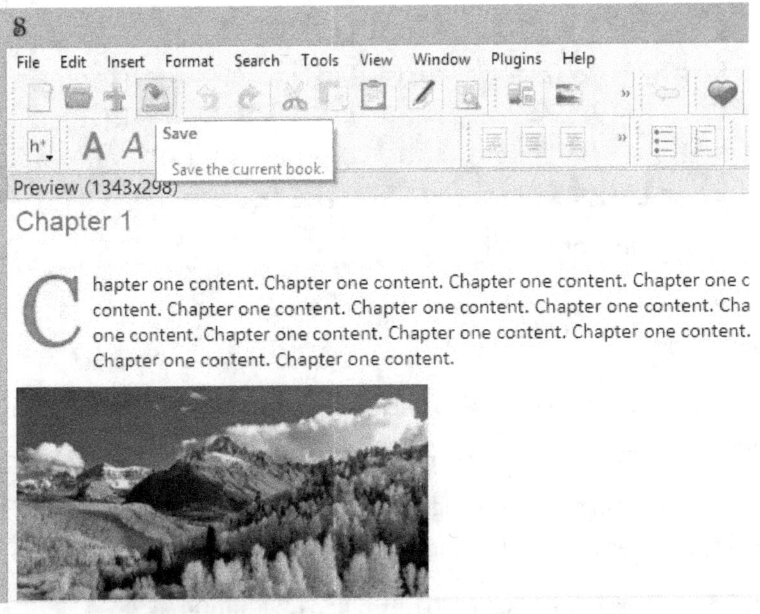

Figure 104. Save the file.

7. How to Make a Table of Contents

The table of contents of an ebook should be like a website menu. That is, if you click on chapter 3 in the table of contents, then chapter 3 appears automatically on the eBook page. This is easy to do, but it takes a lot of time if your book has many chapters. My demo book has only 3 chapters.

Open the book at the table of contents and look at the HTML code. (Fig. 105).

```
<p class="block_3">Table of contents</p>
<p class="block_1">Chapter 1</p>
<p class="block_1">Chapter 2</p>
<p class="block_1">Chapter 3</p>
<p class="block_1">About the author</p>
    <p class="break_1"> </p>
```

Figure 105. Table of contents code.

Remove all unnecessary HTML tags and leave only paragraph tags as shown above.

Then add an additional code to each chapter. But first, you must check on which HTML file each chapter starts.

If chapter one starts on the page index_split_001.html then the code for the first chapter is the following:

<a href="../Text/index_split_001.html#ch1">Chapter 1</a>

If Chapter two starts on the page index_split_002.html then the code for Chapter 2 is as follows:

<a href="../Text/index_split_002.html#ch2">Chapter 2</a> And so on. (Fig. 106)

```
titlepage.xhtml    index_split_000.html    stylesheet.css    index_split_001.html
17     <p class="block_3">Table of contents</p>
18 <p class="block_1">
19 <a href="../Text/index_split_001.html#ch1">Chapter 1</a>
20 </p>
21 <p class="block_1">
22 <a href="../Text/index_split_002.html#ch2">Chapter 2</a>
23 </p>
24 <p class="block_1">
25 <a href="../Text/index_split_003.html#ch3">Chapter 3</a>
26 </p>
27 <p class="block_1">
28 <a href="../Text/index_split_003.html#ch4">About the
```

Figure 106. Table of contents code

Now add the code to the title of each chapter in the text of the book. If in the Table of Contents, the title of the chapter has the code <a href="…/Text/index_split_001.html #ch1"> Chapter Title </a>, then in the text of the book, the title of the chapter should have this code:

<a id="ch1"> Chapter Title </a>

Any code can be used in place of "ch1". It is only important that it starts with a letter, and not with a number, and it must be the same for the title in the Table of Contents and for the title in the text of the book.

To the code of Chapter 1 in the text of the book:

<h2 class="block_4">Chapter 1</h2>

Add this code:

<h2 class="block_4"><a id="ch1">Chapter 1 </a></h2>

Figure 107. Change the title code of Chapter 1 in the text of the book.

To the code of Chapter 2 in the text of the book:

<h2 class="block_4">Chapter 2</h2>

Add this code:

<h2 class="block_4"><a id="ch2">Chapter 2 </a></h2>

Figure 108. Change the title code of Chapter 2 in the text of the book.

To the code of Chapter 3 in the text of the book:

<h2 class="block_4">Chapter 3</h2>

Add this code:

<h2 class="block_4"><a id="ch3">Chapter 3 </a></h2>

Figure 109. Change the title code of Chapter 3 in the text of the book.

I will repeat once again: if in the Table of Contents, the title of the chapter has the code <a href="…#ch1"> Title </a>, then in the text of the book, the title of the chapter should have the following code:
<a id="ch1"> Title </a>.

Moreover, in place of "ch1" any code can be used. It is only important that it starts with a letter, and not with a number, and it must be the same for the title in the Table of Contents and for the title in the text of the book.

For the Table of Contents to work, you need to edit the toc.ncx file.

```
<navPoint class="chapter" id="num_1" playOrder="1">
  <navLabel>
    <text>Chapter 1</text>
  </navLabel>
  <content src="Text/index_split_001.html#ch1"/>
</navPoint>
<navPoint class="chapter" id="num_2" playOrder="2">
  <navLabel>
    <text>Chapter 2</text>
  </navLabel>
  <content src="Text/index_split_002.html#ch2"/>
</navPoint>
```

Figure 110. The toc.ncx file

A code must exist for each chapter in the toc.ncx file, as in the Figure 110 between the <navPoint> and </navPoint> tags.

It is important to understand what the <content src=Text/index_split_001.html#ch1"/> string means:

"Text" is the name of the folder where the text files are located.

HTML files are the book text files. In your case, the files for the chapters may have different names, then the same file names should be on the line for each chapter. If Chapter 1 starts on the index_split_001.html file then the same file must be used in the content src string. If Chapter 2 starts on the index_split_002.html file then the same file must be used in the content src string. (Fig. 111).

```
13    <navMap>
14      <navPoint class="chapter" id="num_1" playOrder="1">
15        <navLabel>
16          <text>Chapter 1</text>
17        </navLabel>
18        <content src="Text/index_split_001.html#ch1"/>
19      </navPoint>
20      <navPoint class="chapter" id="num_2" playOrder="2">
21        <navLabel>
22          <text>Chapter 2</text>
23        </navLabel>
24        <content src="Text/index_split_002.html#ch2"/>
25      </navPoint>
26      <navPoint class="chapter" id="num_3" playOrder="3">
27        <navLabel>
28          <text>Chapter 3</text>
29        </navLabel>
30        <content src="Text/index_split_003.html#ch3"/>
31      </navPoint>
32      <navPoint class="chapter" id="num_4" playOrder="4">
33        <navLabel>
34          <text>About the author</text>
35        </navLabel>
36        <content src="Text/index_split_003.html#ch4"/>
37      </navPoint>
```

Figure 111. toc.ncx file. The content tag is different for each chapter.

ch1, # ch2 and # ch3 are indices of chapters of a book.

In the toc.ncx file, the content code for different chapters will be different. For example, for Chapter 1, whose title is located on the index_split_001.html file, the content code will contain the index_split_001.html file.

And for Chapter 2, whose title is located on the index_split_002.html file, the content code will contain the index_split_002.html file.

And for Chapter 3, whose title is located on the index_split_003.html file, the content code will contain the index_split_003.html file.

"About the author" title is located on the index_split_003.html file, then the content code will contain the index_split_003.html file.

8. Mistakes You can Make in Epub Code

What mistakes can you make in the EPUB code? Imagine, you corrected a paragraph and accidentally deleted the end tag of a paragraph: </p>. (Fig. 112)

For the EPUB model of the book, I used fake text: a repeating sentence: "Chapter one content" for the first chapter, "Chapter two content" for the second chapter and "Chapter three content" for the third chapter.

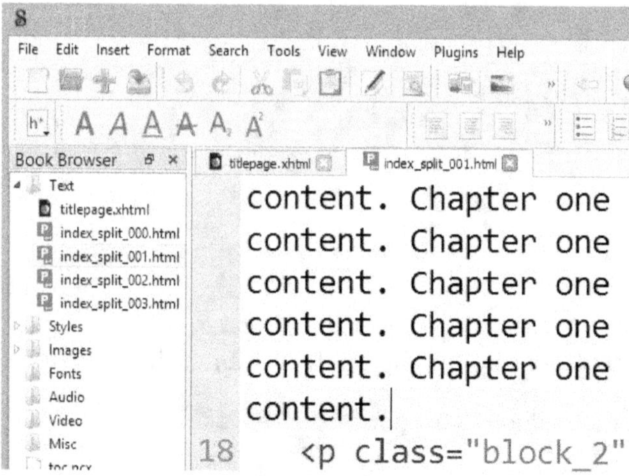

Figure 112. The end tag of a paragraph is missing.

If you try to save the EPUB, it will display an error: (Fig. 113).

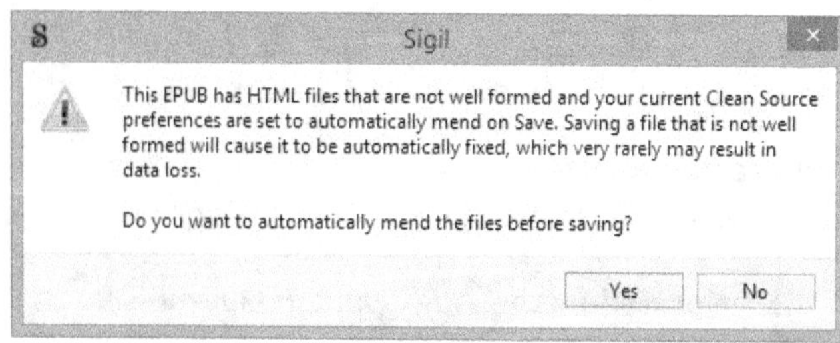

Figure 113. An error was found.

Click No, to fix the error manually.

From the main menu select View, Preview

The preview of the page will display the error message. See Figure 114.

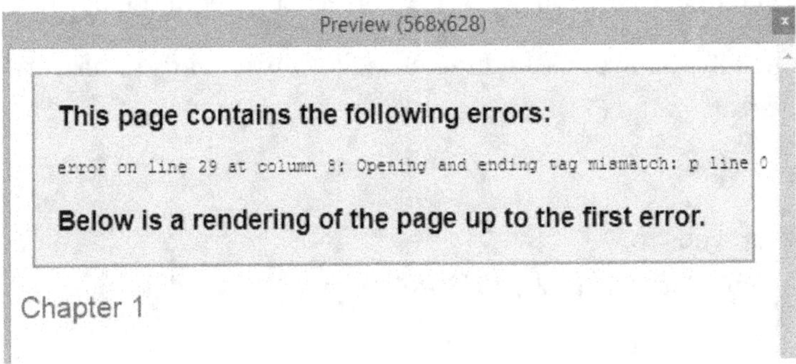

Figure 114. Error on line 29 at column 8.

In Figure 114, you will see that a paragraph with the missing end paragraph tag starts on line 17 but the message says that the error is located on line 29. It is confusing. If you count each line from the top of the file then you will see that the missing end tag is located indeed on line 29.

So, you can find the line and fix the error by entering the end paragraph tag: </p>.

Remember that each tag is a pair: start tag and end tag. For example, a paragraph has <p> and </p> tags, a span tag has a <span> beginning and a </span> end tag. The link tag has a beginning <a ......> and an end </a> tag.

9. Epub Validation

You have created a table of contents. Click on each chapter in the table of contents and make sure you get to the correct chapter in the book.

Congratulations! You have finished the e-book! Now it needs to be checked for errors in the EPUB validator.

See Figures 115 and 116.

EPUB Validator website:
https://www.ebookit.com/tools/bp/Bo/eBookIt/EPUB-validator

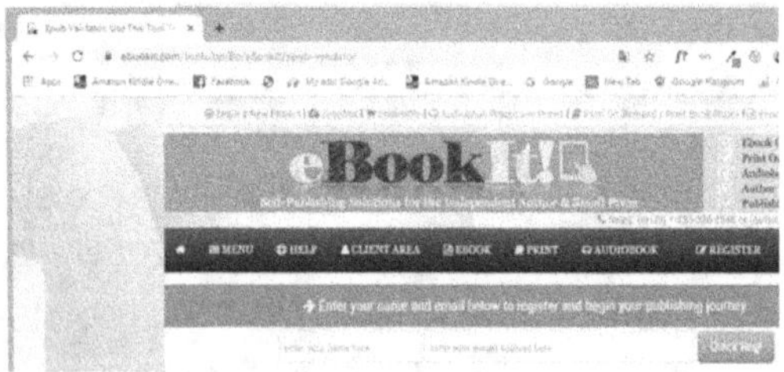

Figure 115. EPUB Validator website.

Go to the bottom of the webpage and click on the link selecting a file.
 (Fig. 116).
A window for selecting files will open. Locate your EPUB file and click the Open button.
The file will be uploaded to the website, and if you did everything correctly, a success message will appear.

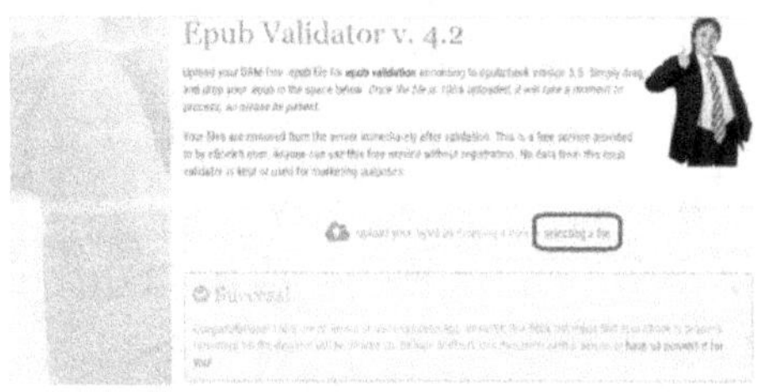

Figure 116. EPUB Validator website. Success! There are no errors!

And if you had made a typo in the code, an error would appear. And the validator will indicate in which file and in which line the error is present. I intentionally made a mistake to demonstrate to you how to fix it. (Fig. 117).

```
11      <text>Lost in The Fall</text>
12   </docTitle>
13   <navMap>
14     <navPoint class="chapter" id="num_1" playOrder="1">
15       <navLabel>
16         <text>Chapter 1</text>
17       </navLabel>
18       <content src="Text/index_split_001.html#ch10"/>
19     </navPoint>
20     <navPoint class="chapter" id="num_2" playOrder="2">
21       <navLabel>
22         <text>Chapter 2</text>
```

Figure 117. On line 18, the code for the first chapter is incorrect: ch10 instead of ch1.

Now save the file and check it for errors in the validator. The validator reports an error. (Fig. 118).

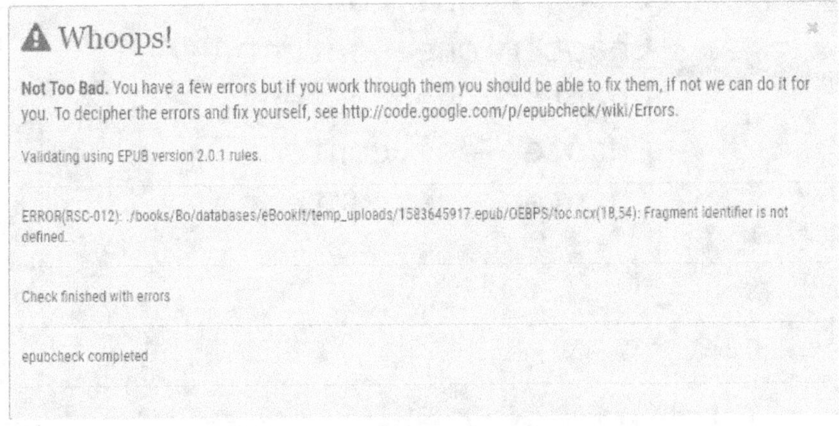

Figure 118. ERROR(RSC012):../books/Bo/database/

eBookkit/temp_updates/1572191008.epub/OEBPS/toc.ncx (18.54):

Fragment identifier is not defined.

The error is in the toc.ncx file on line 18 and on the letter 54. The chapter code is not defined. (Fig. 119).

In the Table of Contents, the code ch1 was used for Chapter 1, so the code ch10 is not recognized.

Change ch10 to ch1, save the file and try uploading it to the validator again. You will receive a message - Success.

In the chapter header an element such as ID may be present:

<h1 class = "block_3" id = "toc_id_1" lang = "ru">

These IDs must be unique. Duplicates cause an error. To avoid such an error, delete all id = "toc_id_" elements. They are not needed. To find all occurrences of the id="toc_id", you can use the Find button. (Fig. 119)

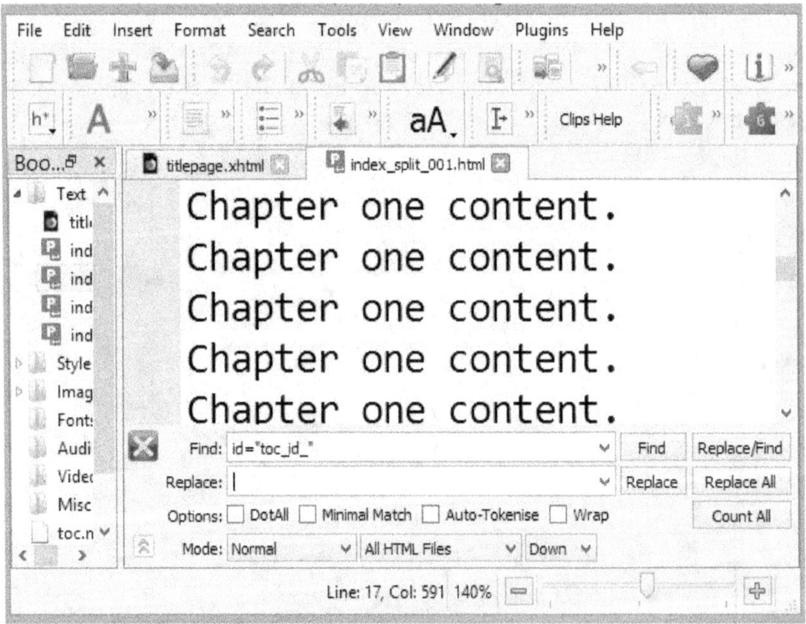

Figure 119. Find all occurrences of id="toc_id_" and replace with empty string. You checked the book in the EPUB validator, and the validation was successful.

10. Drop Cap

I have prepared a bonus for you. In Figure 120, you see that the first letter of the first line of the new chapter is much larger in size than all the other letters and it creates a special effect. I will show you the CSS code that will make the first letter bigger.

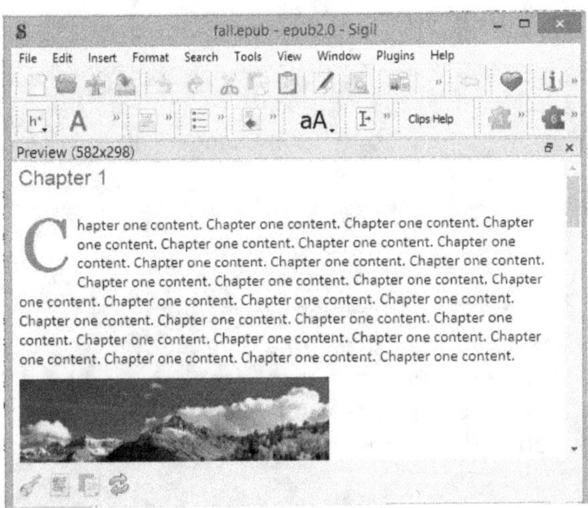

Figure 120. Drop cap

Open the stylesheet.css file and create a new class with the name of dropcap, as shown in Figure 121.

```
124 .dropcap {
125 color: #ff0000;
126 float: left;
127 font-family: Georgia;
128 font-size: 75px;
129 line-height: 60px;
130 padding-top: 0px;
131 padding-right: 8px;
132 padding-left: 3px;
133 padding-bottom:0px;
134 }
```

Figure 121. A CSS code for the dropcap class. (A class in CSS must have a dot in front of its name.)

In the text of the book, place the first letter of each chapter in the   tag, as shown in Figure 122.

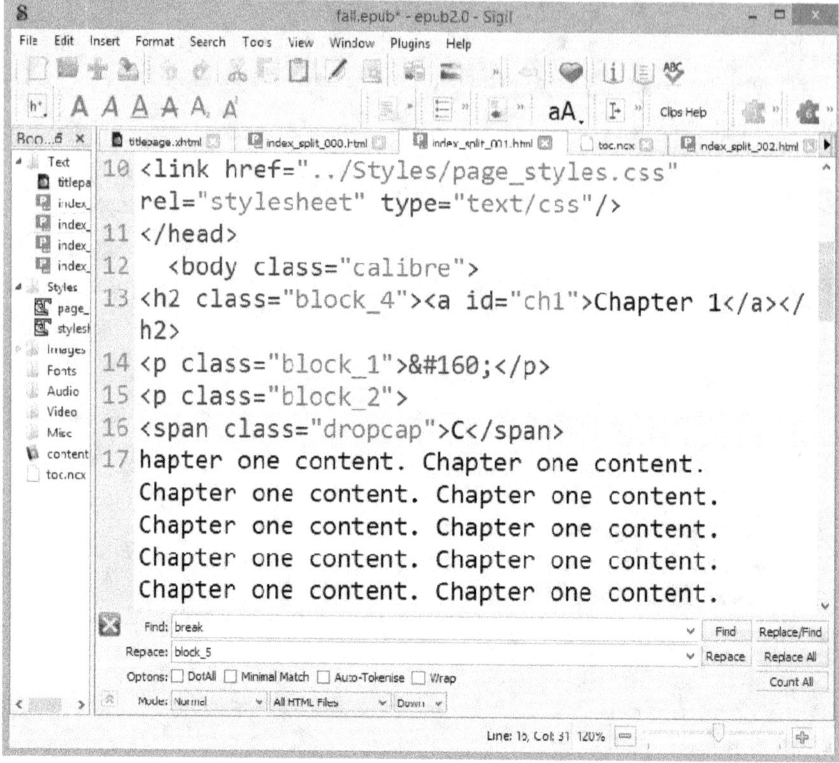

Figure 122. Drop Cap letter. HTML code.

Save the EPUB file and open it in the Calibre e-book viewer.

To open it, select your EPUB file with the right mouse button and select "Open with" in the drop-down menu.

From the list of applications select the calibre e-book viewer. (Fig. 123)

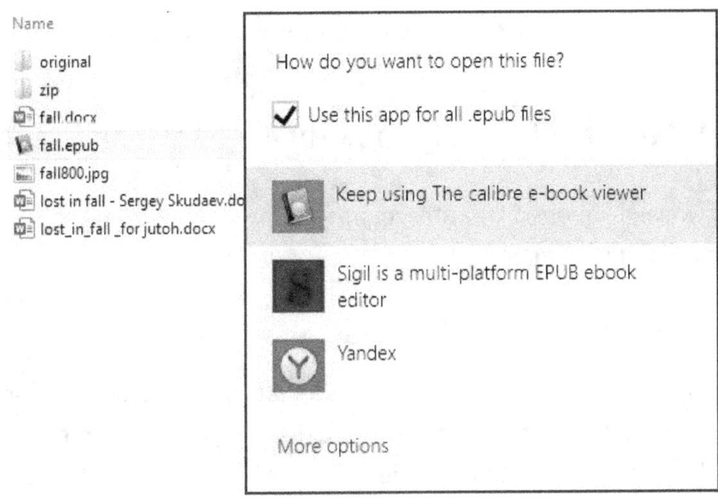

Figure 123. Open EPUB in calibre e-book viewer.

Try to click each entry in the table of contents to make sure the links are correct, and the correct chapter is displayed.

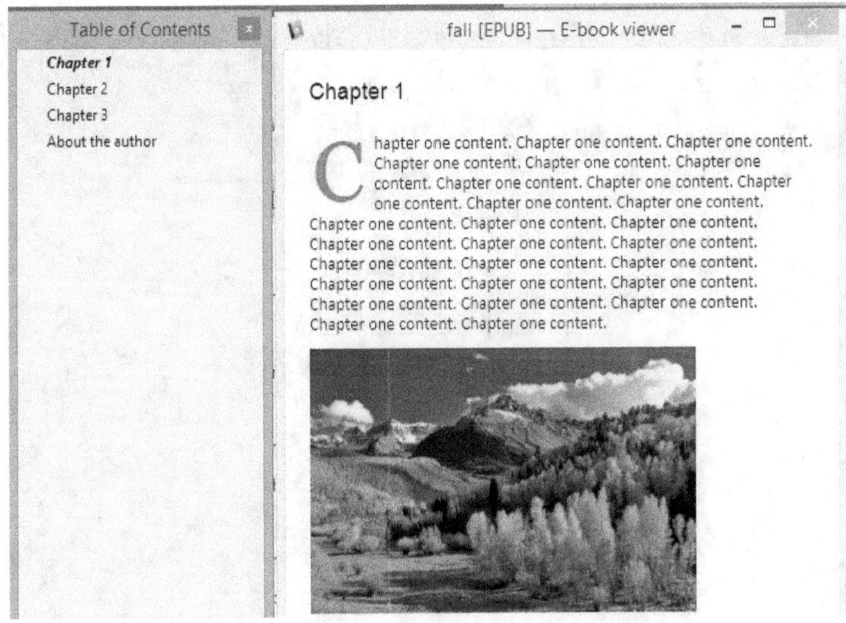

Figure 124.eBook is opened in calibre e-book viewer. Chapter 1.

You see that the first character of the chapter is much bigger than the main text.

11. How to Use Jutoh to Format Your Book

Jutohis software developed by anthemion software ltd based in the UK. you can download it from

http://www.jutoh.com/download.htm.

With Jutoh you can create two types of EPUB files: flow layout and fixed layout. The flow layout does not contain the fixed pages. The contents of the file flows freely depending on device screen size. The fixed layout EPUB file has fixed page width and height. Fixed layout is used for a picture eBook or children's books. So far we have only discussed flow layout in EPUB format.

11.1. How to Create Reflowable Layout Epub with Jutoh

Start Jutoh and from the main menu select File, New Project (Fig. 125)

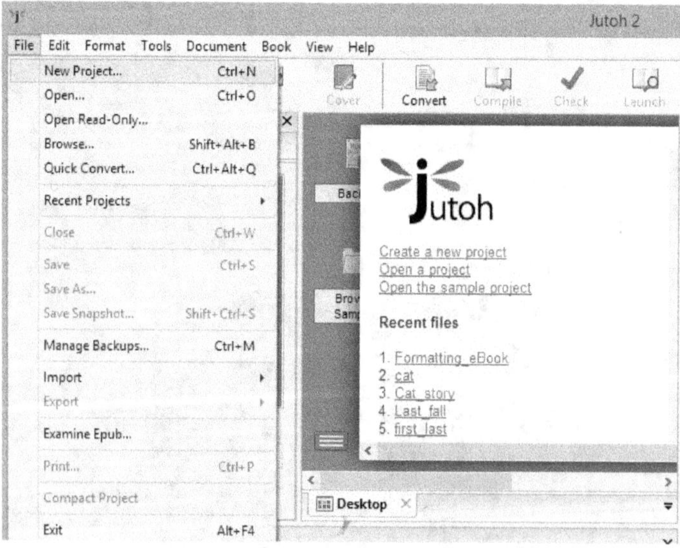

Figure 125. Create a new project.

In the next window fill in the book title, author name, publisher, description etc. (Fig. 126)

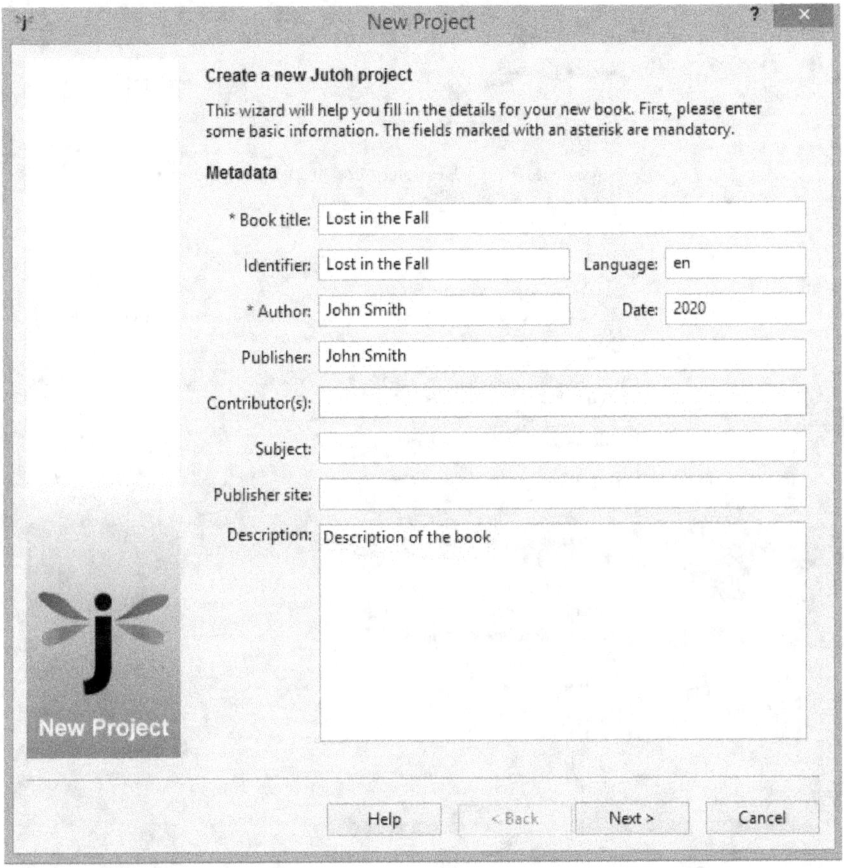

Figure 126. A project metadata.

Click the Next button.

In the next window select the eBook format. For example, epub and Mobipocket. (Fig. 127)

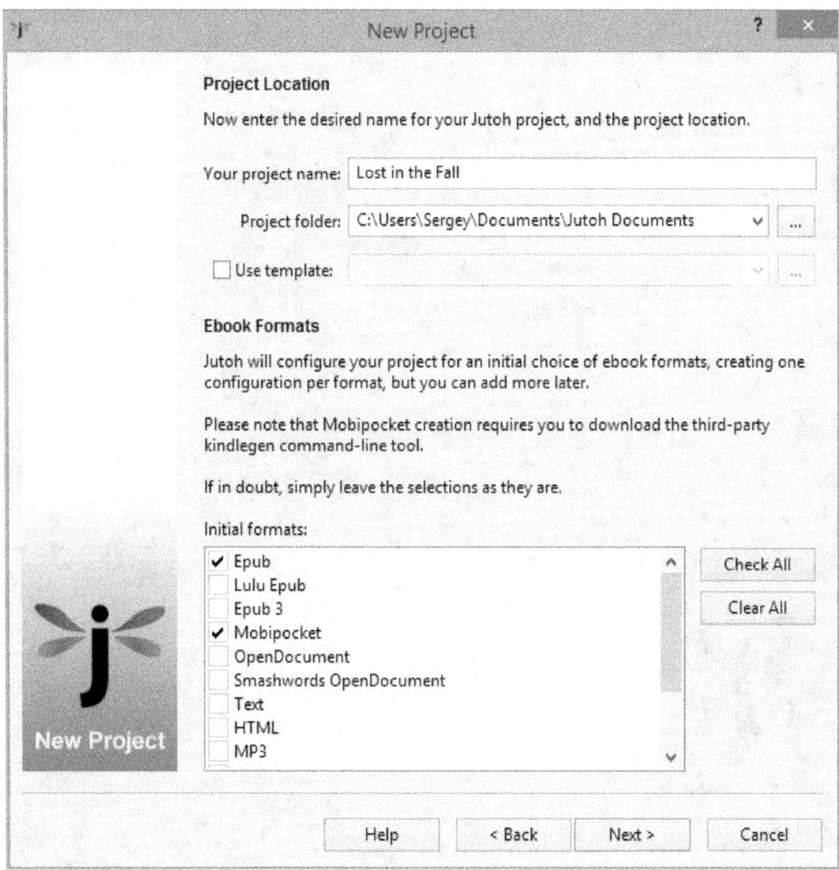

Figure 127. Click the Next button.

In the next window select epub type: reflowable or fixed layout. For a regular book select reflowable type. (Fig.128)

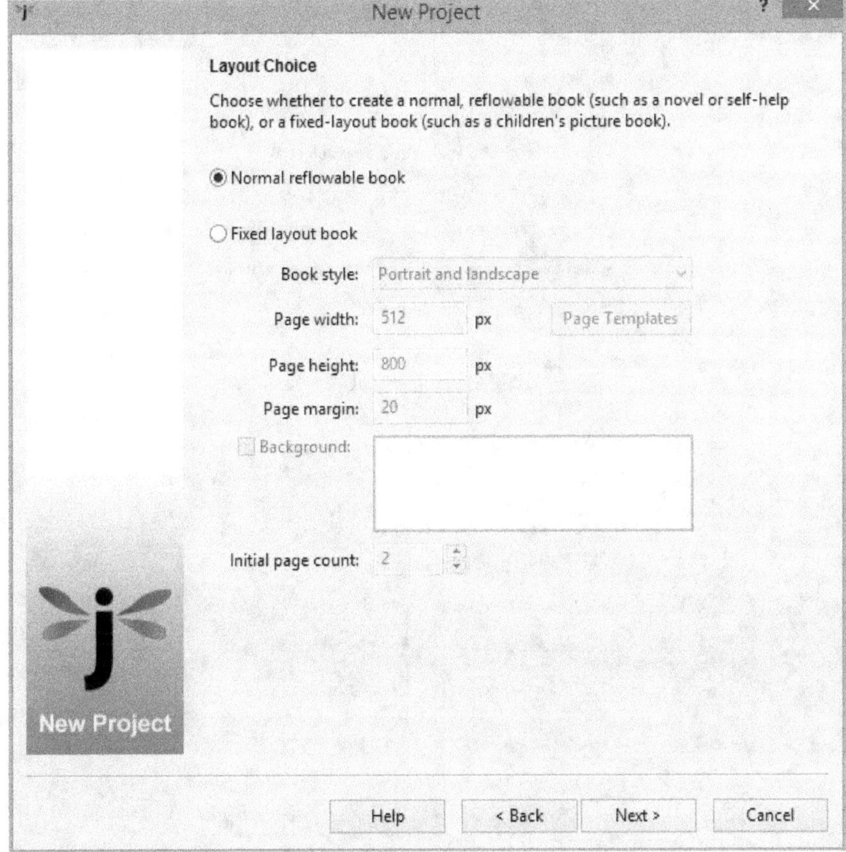

Figure 128. Normal reflowable book.

Click the Next button.

In the next window select import images if your book has any. Set maximum image width 800px.

Select Create standard style sheet. Leave the rest as it is. (Fig.129)

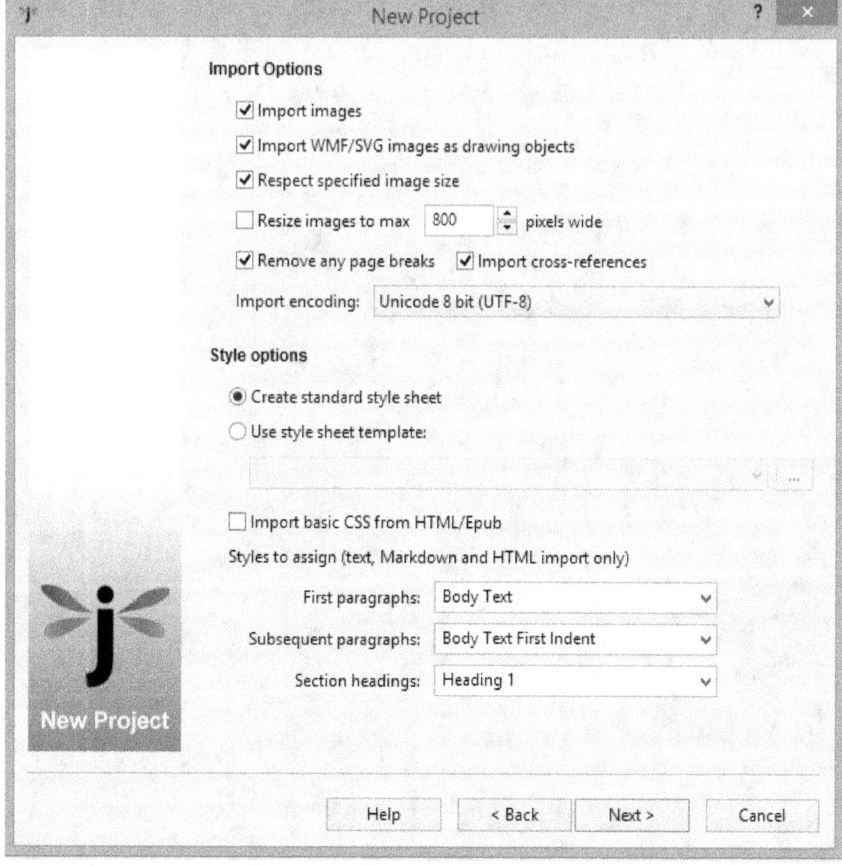

Figure 129. Images and style sheets.

Click the Next button.

In the next window, mark "From an existing file containing all sections". Click the Browse button and select your word document. (Fig.130)

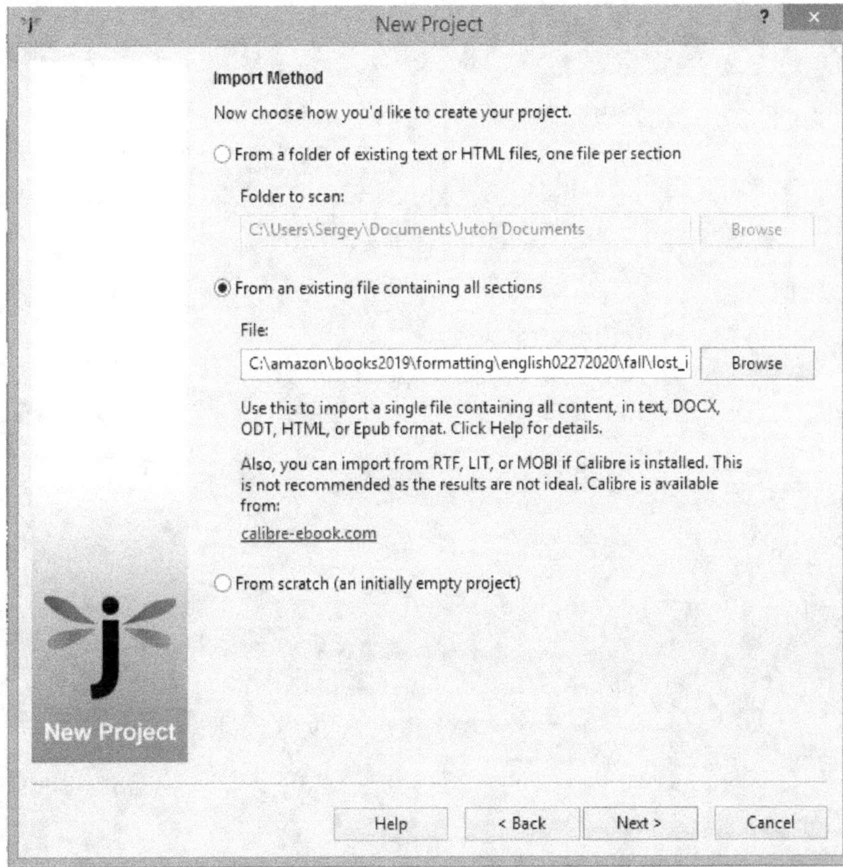

Figure 130. Select a work document.

Click the Next button.

In the next window select how to split your book into chapters. Remember, Heading 2 was used for chapter titles.

And Heading 2 must not be used for any other element of your manuscript. For example, for author name etc.

If Heading 2 is used only for chapter titles then the book will be split into chapters correctly.

In the next window you can see that the demo book was split correctly into 3 chapters and author bio. (Fig.131)

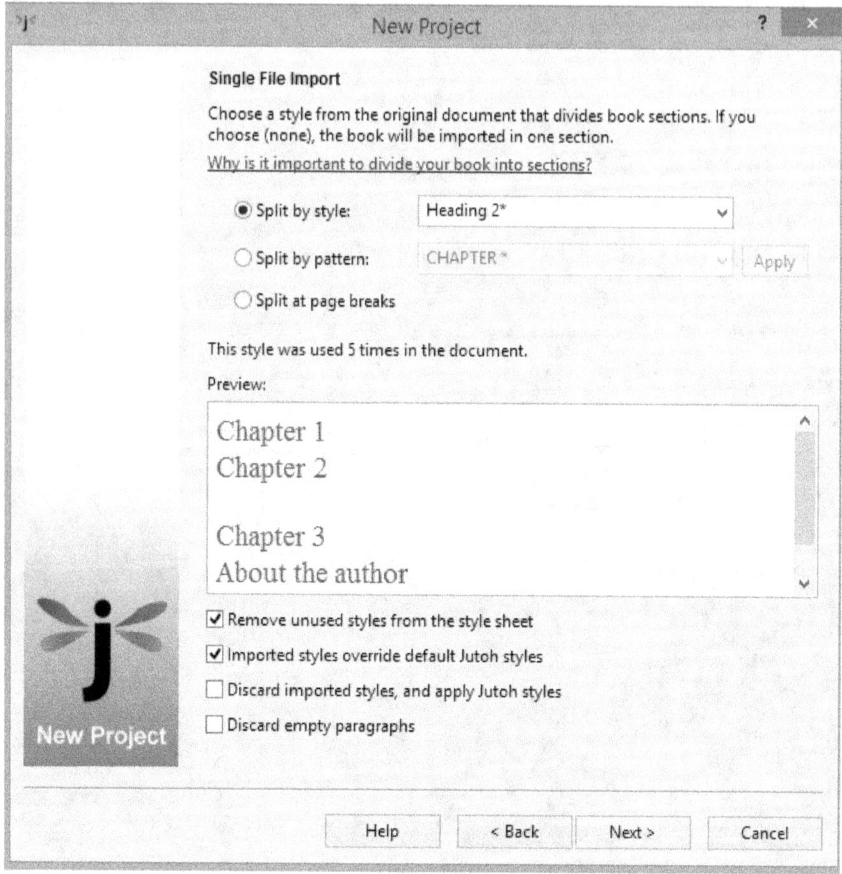

Figure 131. The document is split into chapters by Heading 2.

Mark the "Discard empty paragraphs" checkbox. Empty paragraphs create blank areas in the ebook.

Click the Next button.

In the next window mark "Use an existing file" for your book cover. Click the Browse button and select the cover image. (Fig.132)

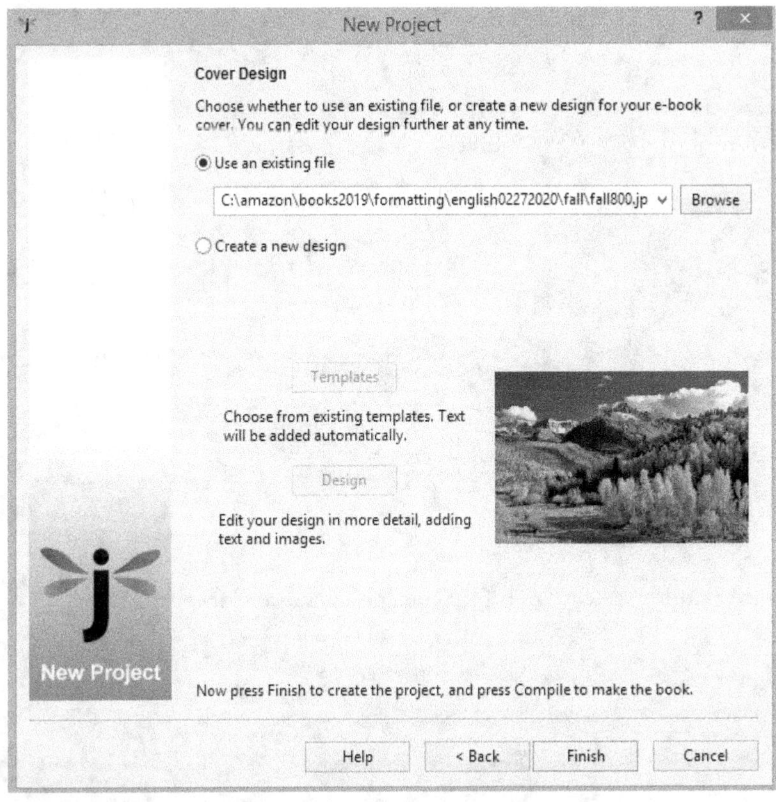

Figure 132. Select the cover image.
Click the Next button. The project will be created. (Fig.133)

Figure 133. Creating Project.

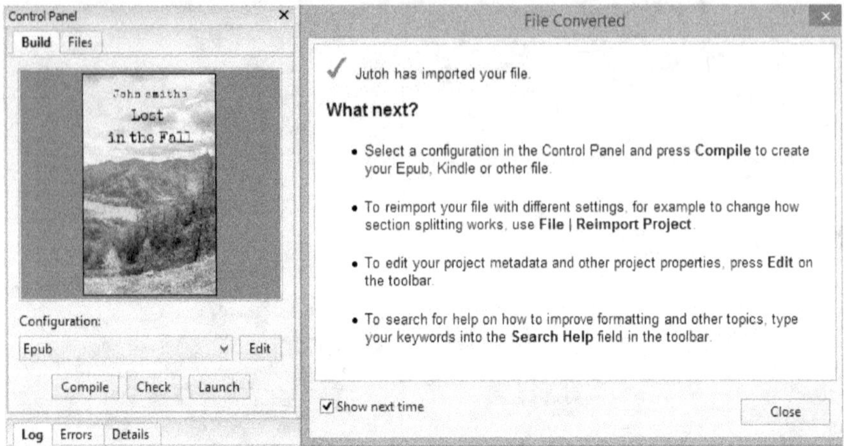

Figure 134. Project is created.

In the next window select epub file type and click the Compile button.
(Fig. 135)

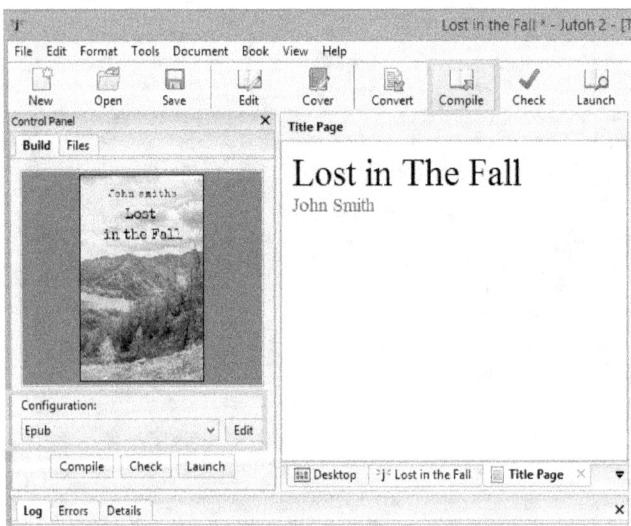

Figure 135. Compile Epub.

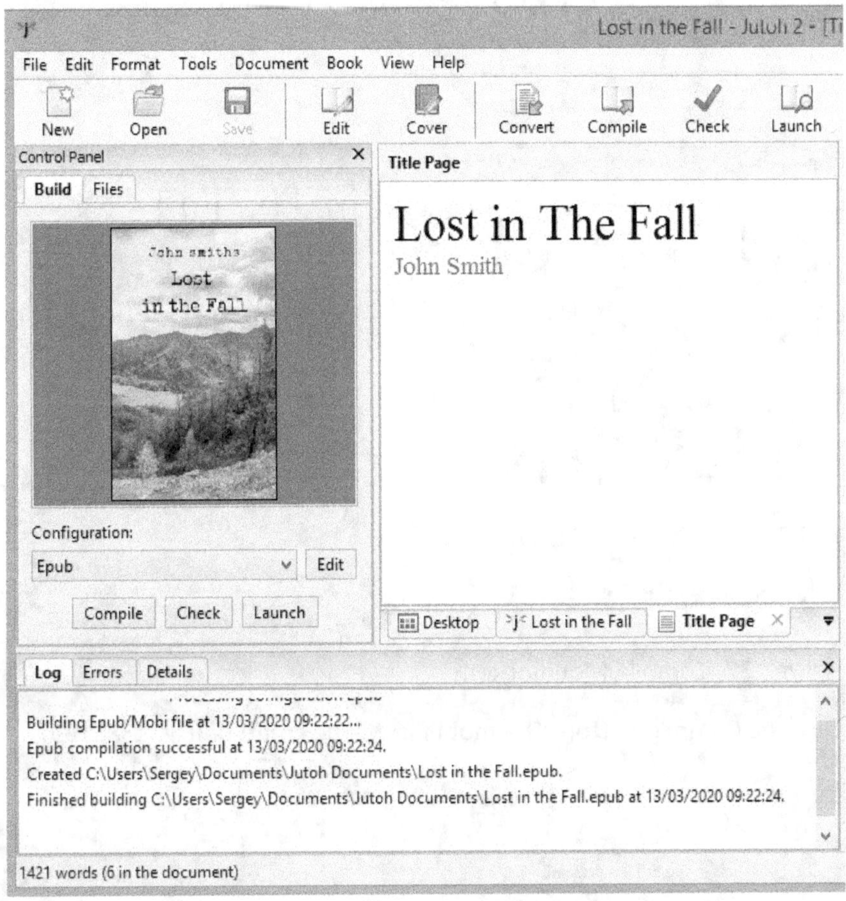

Figure 136. The epub file is created.

The epub file is created in the "Documents\Jutoh Documents" folder.

Click a drop-down list under the Configuration label and select the Mobipocket file type. (Fig.137)

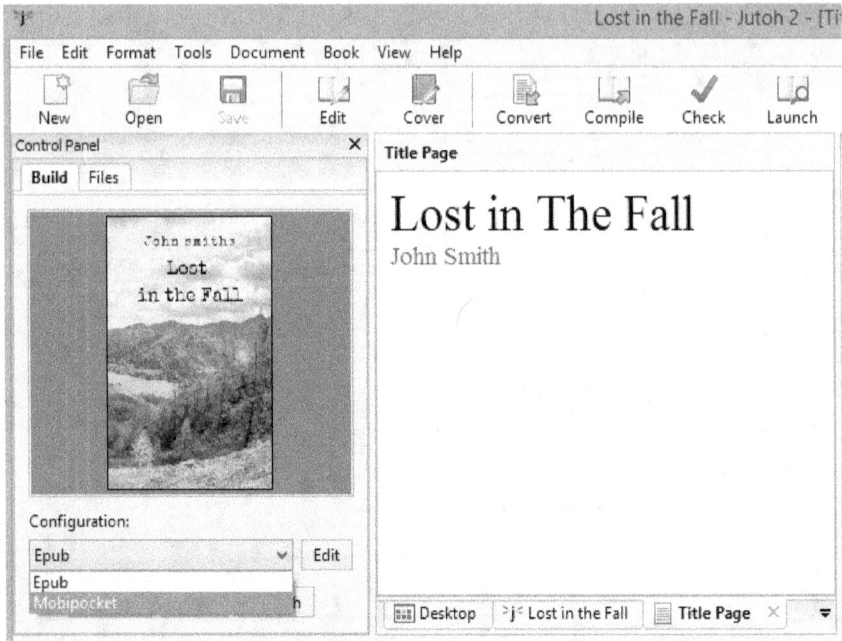

Figure 137. Compile Mobipocket.

Click the Compile button. The mobi file will be created. (Fig. 138, 139)

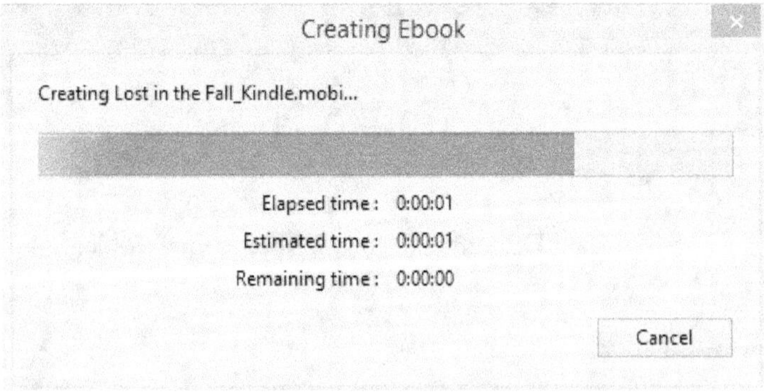

Figure 138. Creating the mobi file.

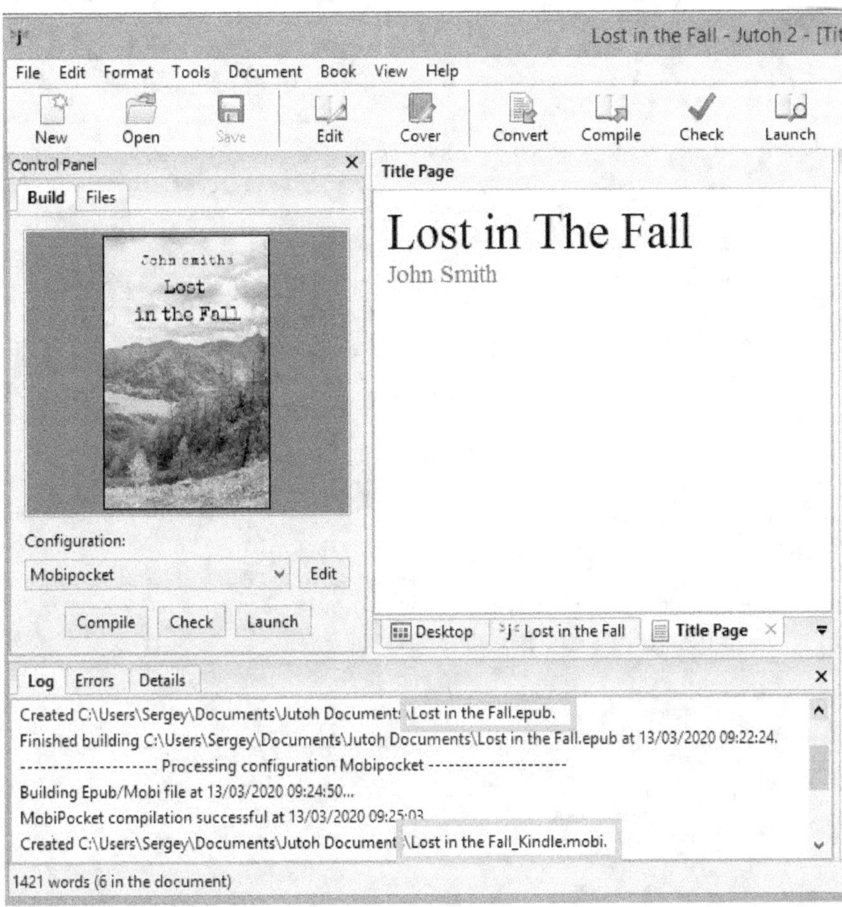

Figure 139. The mobi file is created in the "Documents/Jutoh Documents" folder.

Open Windows Explorer and find the "Documents/Jutoh Documents" folder. (Fig. 140)

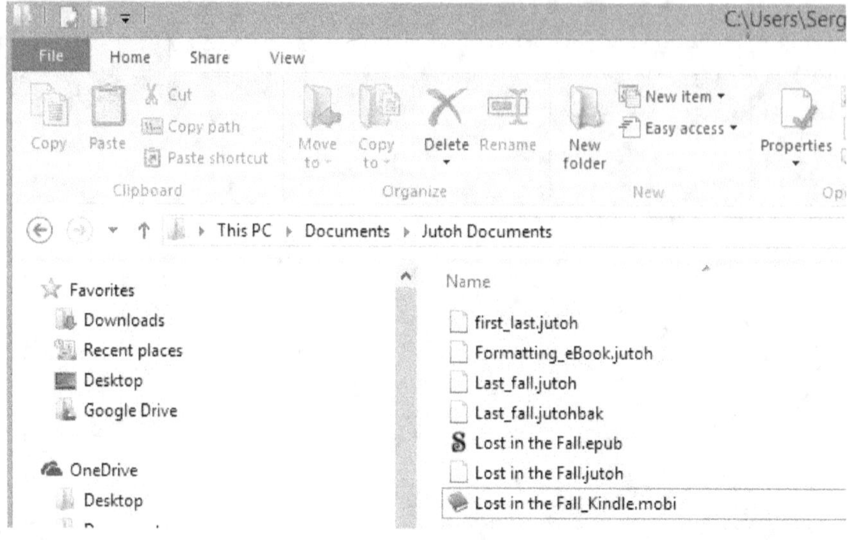

Figure 140. epub and mobi files are created.

Select the epub file and click with the right mouse button. Select Open with. From the list select "The calibre e-book viewer". (Fig. 141)

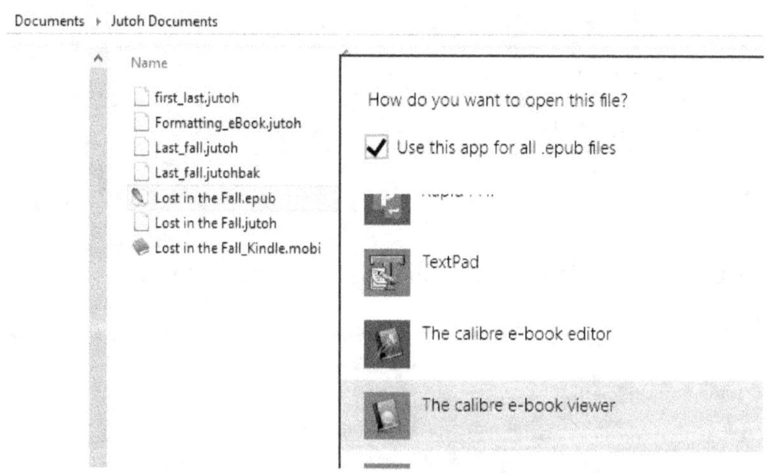

Figure 141. Open epub with calibre e-book viewer.

The epub file is opened. You will see the book cover on the right and the table of contents on the left. (Fig.142)

Figure 142. Epub book is opened in the calibre e-book reader.

In figure 142, you can see the table of contents. Click each chapter and check if the correct chapter is displayed. (Fig.143)

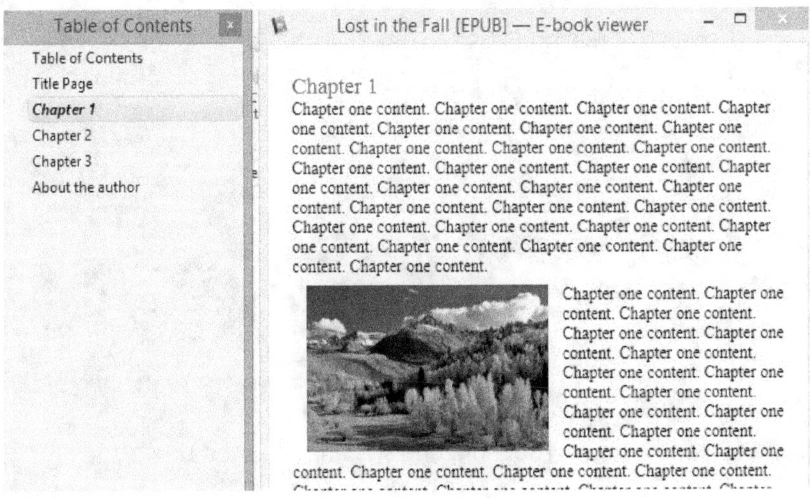

Figure 143. Chapter 1 opened.

To open the mobi file, click it with the right mouse button and select Open with. From the list select Kindle for PC. (Figures 144 and 145)

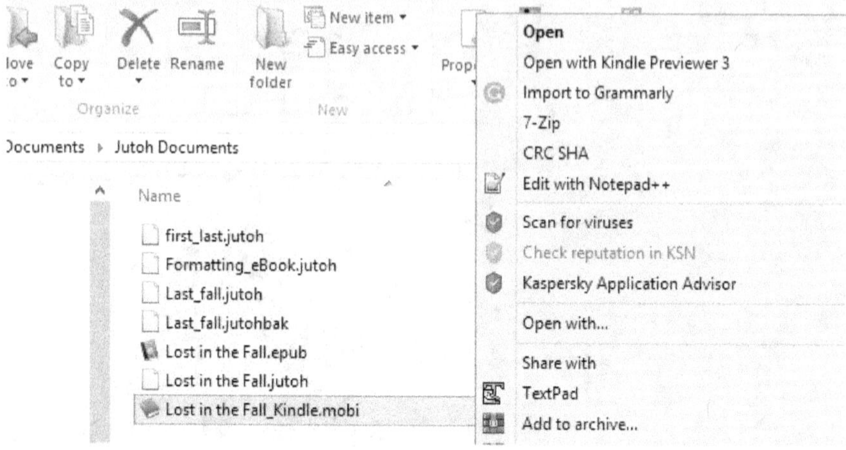

Figure 144. Opening mobi file with Kindle for PC.

The mobi file is opened in Kindle for PC. You will see the table of contents and the page you selected. (Fig. 145)

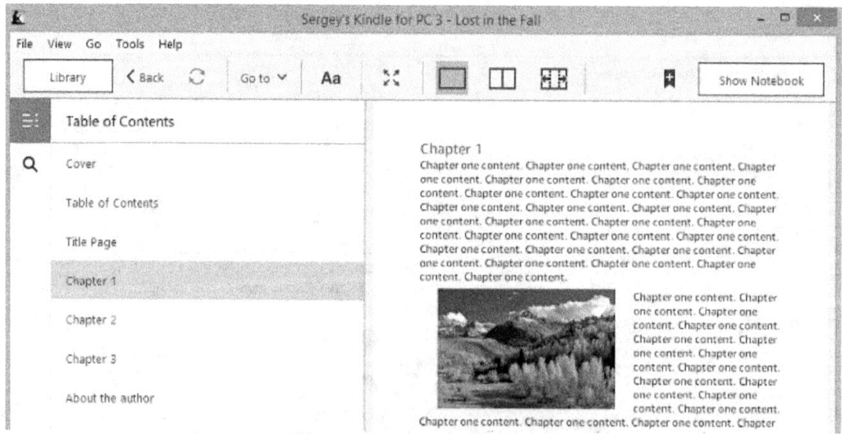

Figure 145. Kindle book. Table of contents and Chapter 1.

Check if the table of contents is working correctly. You can open the automatically created epub file in Sigil and edit it to perfection as we described in chapter 6: How to Edit an EPUB File in the Sigil Program.

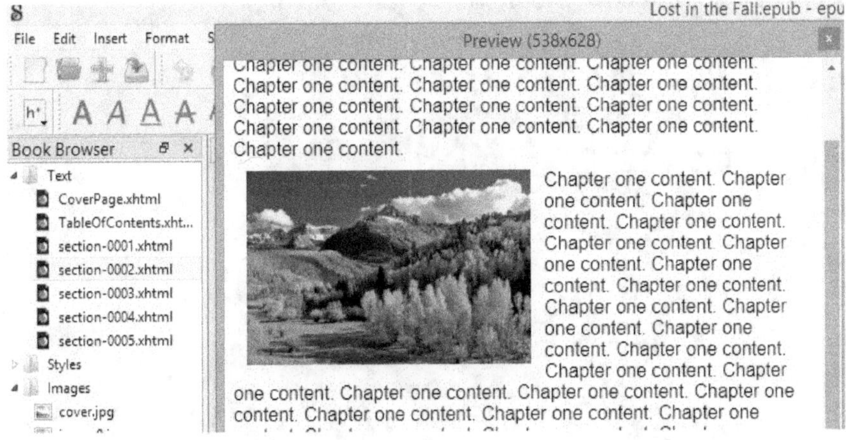

Figure 146. epub book opened in Sigil.

In Figure 146, you see that if the image width is much less than the width of the page, then the text is wrapped around the image. If you have two small images located one after another they may display side by side and their captions may be misplaced. It creates a mess. To avoid this, make images at least 600 pixels wide. Just add white space to the image to make it wider

11.2. Fixed Layout Epub

Fixed layout EPUB is used for photography books or books for children where illustrations are the main content. I will show you step by step, how I created a photography book. Start Jutoh and select a new project as you did for the flow layout book. Enter meta data. (Fig. 147)

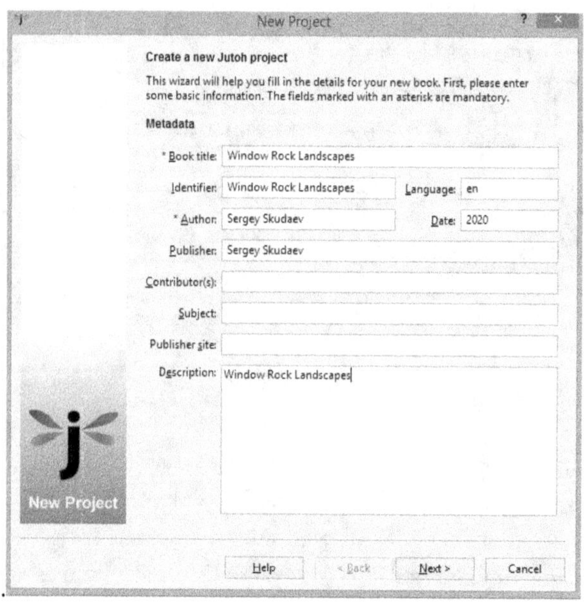

Figure 147. Enter your book's metadata and click the Next button.

In the next window, select Ebook and Mobipocket , as your initial formats. (Fig. 148)

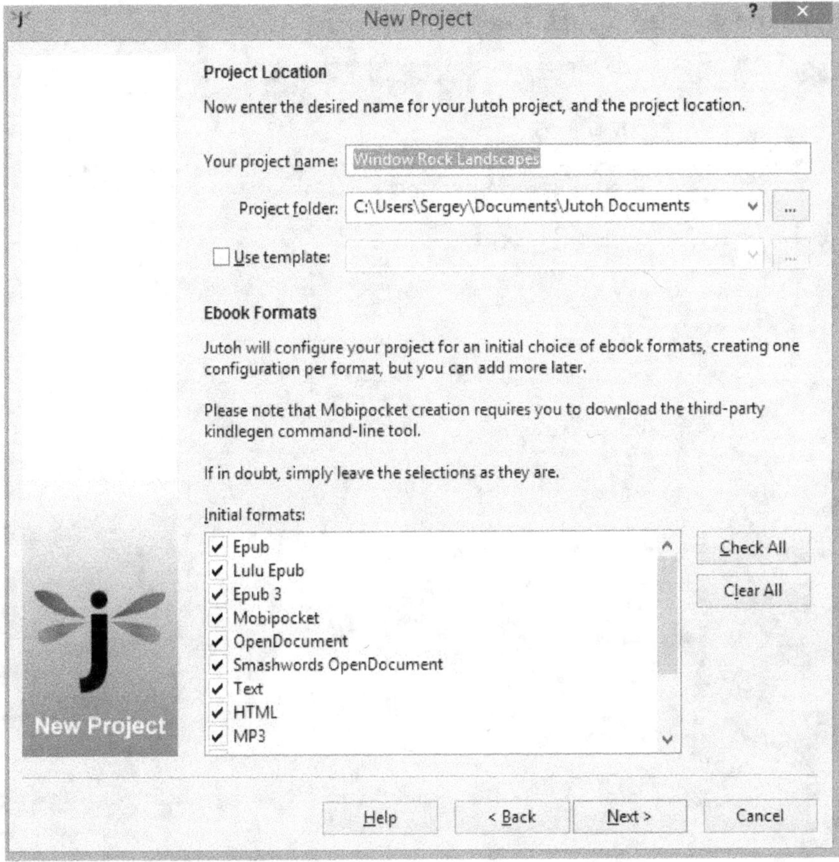

Figure 148. Initial Formats.

Click the Next button. In the next window select "Fixed layout book". Set page size, orientation or select a page template.

Enter the number of pages your book will have. (Fig. 149)

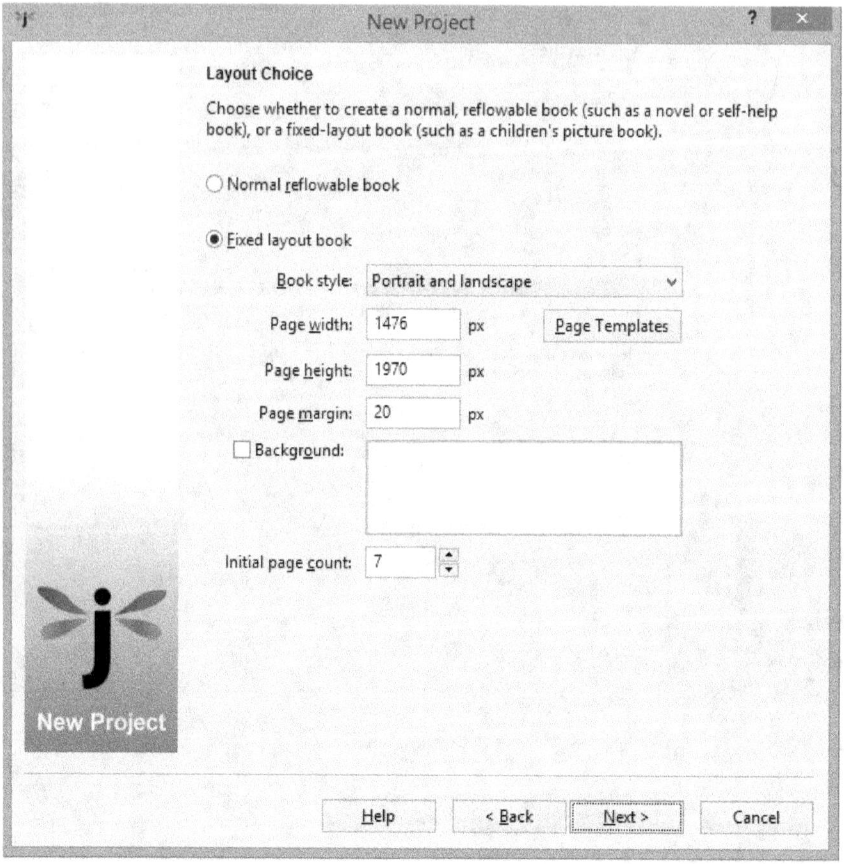

Figure 149. Fixed layout book.

Click the Next button.

In the next window select "From scratch (an initial empty project)" See (Fig. 150)

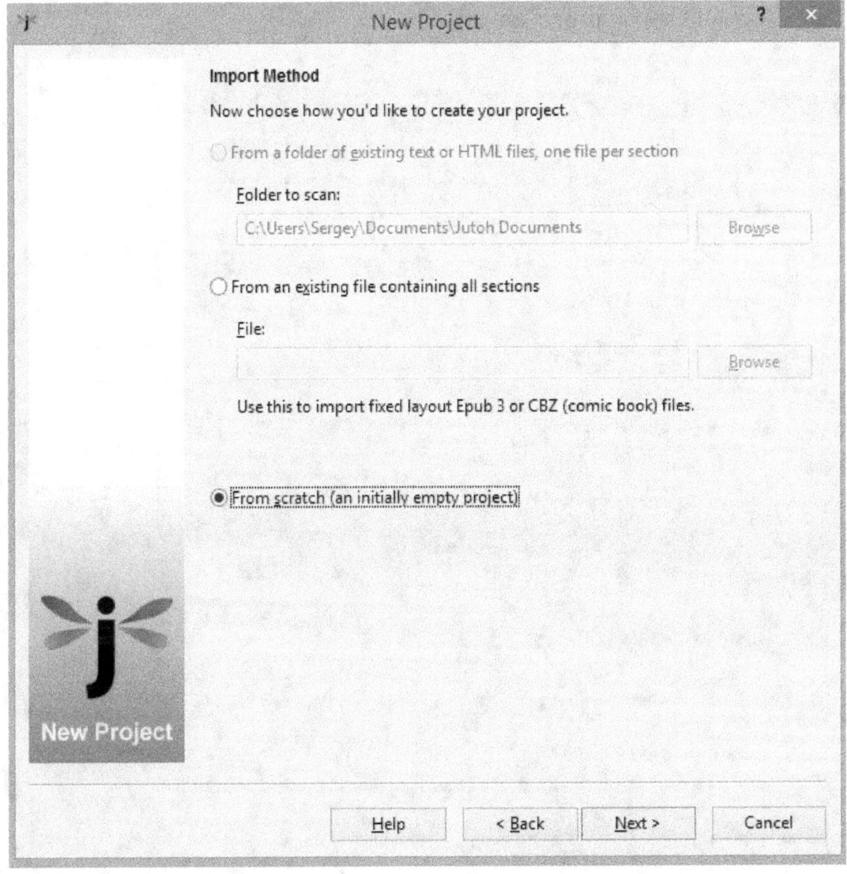

Figure 150. From scratch.

Click the Next button.

In the next window select "Use an existing file" if you have a designed cover. I would recommend having one.(Fig. 151)

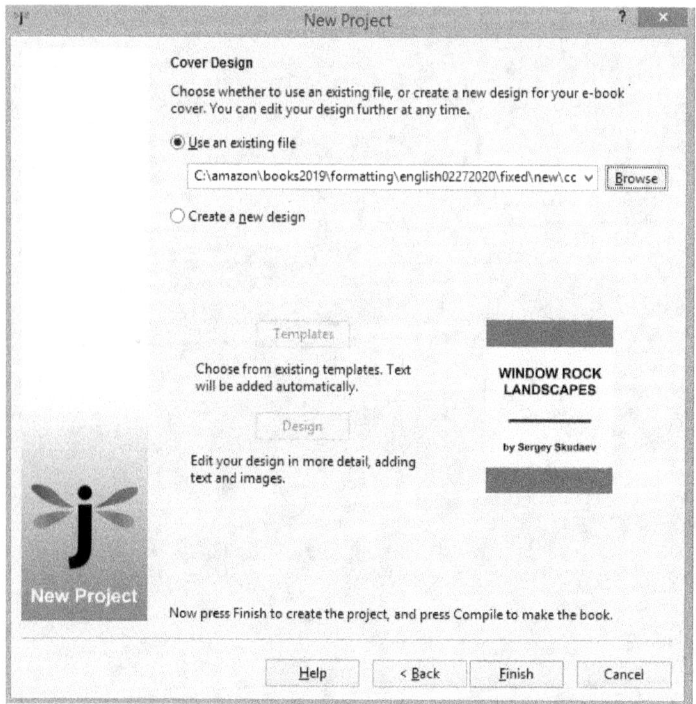

Figure 151. Use an existing file for your book cover.

Select your exiting cover image and click the Next button.

In the next window, you will see a tree with the pages of your book. The first page will be open. (Fig. 152)

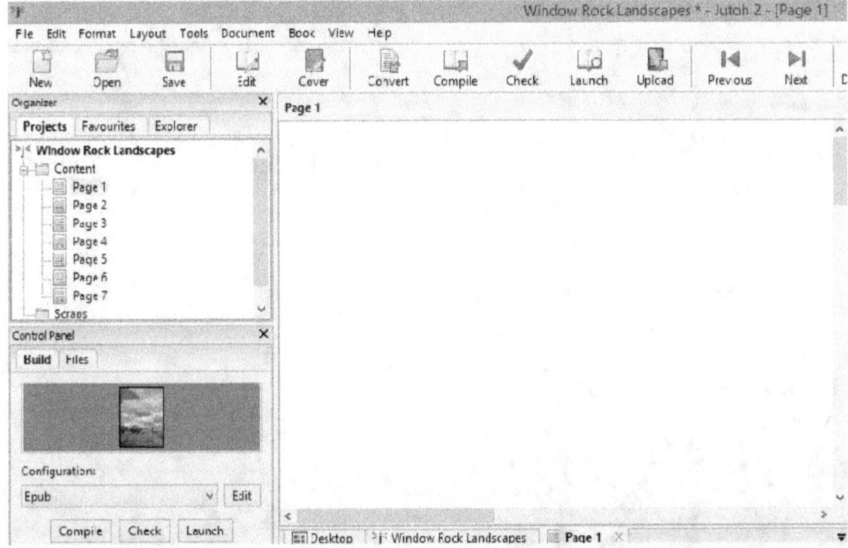

Figure 152. Your book content pages.

To add your image to the page, from the main menu, select Layout, Add Image Object. (Fig. 153)

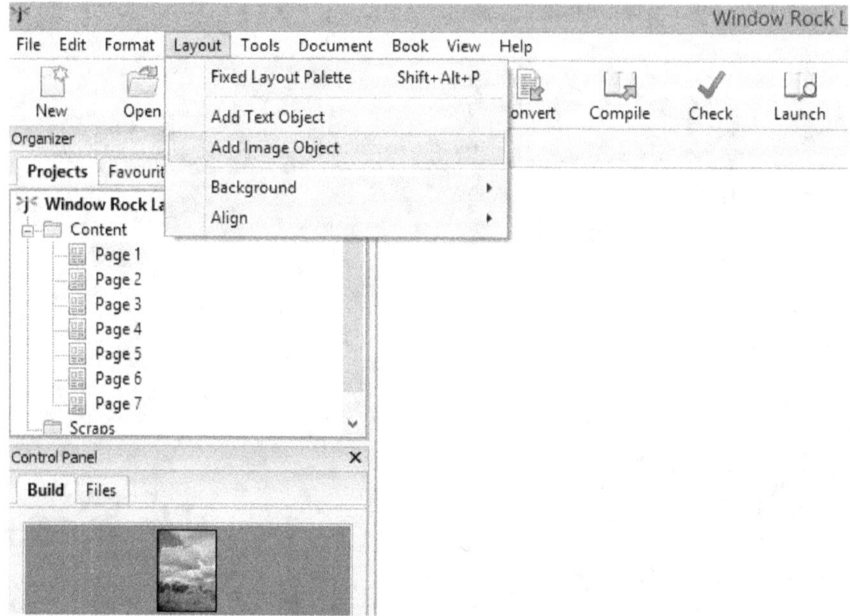

Figure 153. Add Image Object.

Select your first photo image and insert onto the page.

To add the image description, from the main menu, select Add Text Object.

A rectangle appears on the left upper corner. Click the rectangle with the right mouse button and select Properties. (Fig. 154)

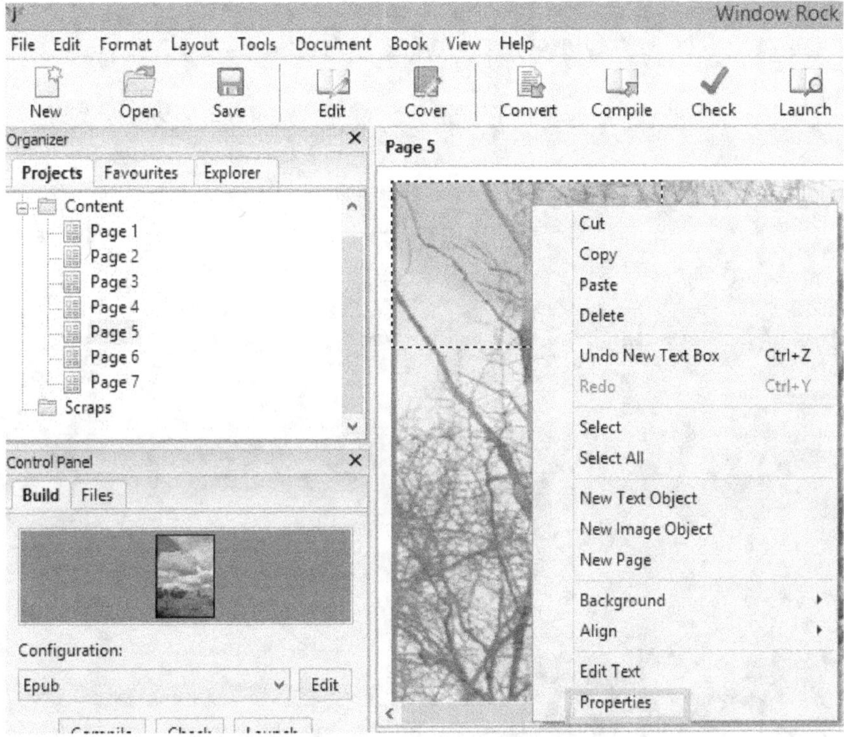

Figure 154. Text Object properties.

In the Object properties window enter pixel numbers in Position. The top position should be greater than your image height. Click the OK button. (Fig. 155)

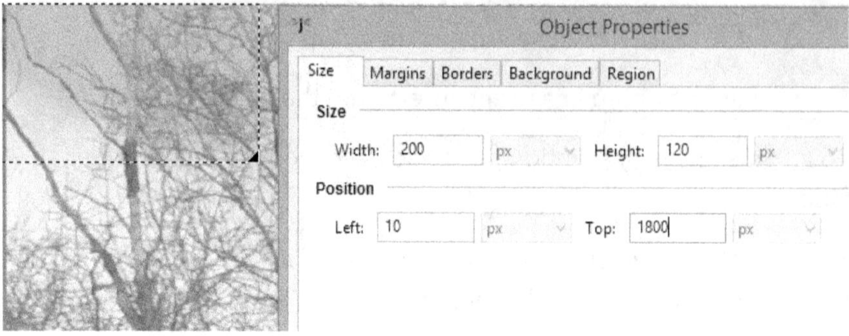

Figure 155. The Text Object position.

Then the text object will be displayed under the picture. (Fig. 156)

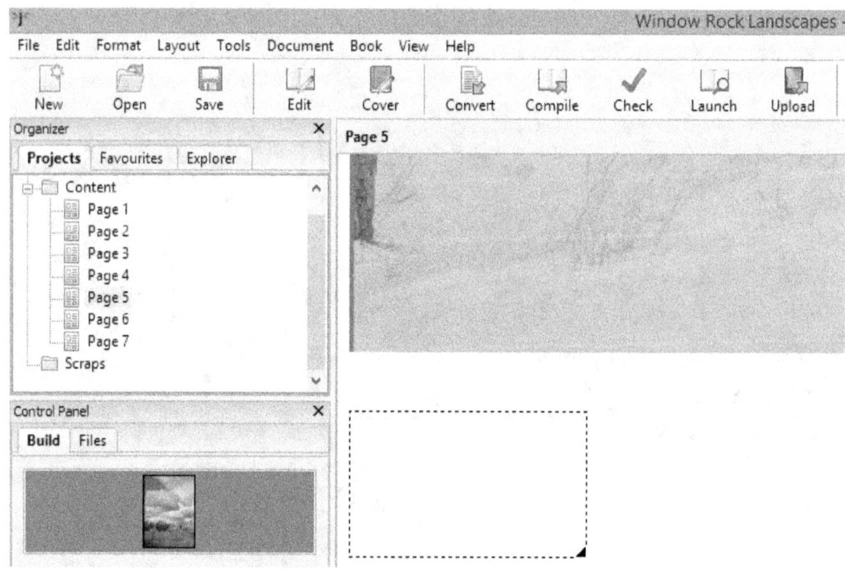

Figure 156. The new text object position.

Add an image and text object to each of your book pages and enter the description of the photographs.

To create an Ebook, in the main menu click the Compile button. The book will be created. (Figs. 157, and 158)

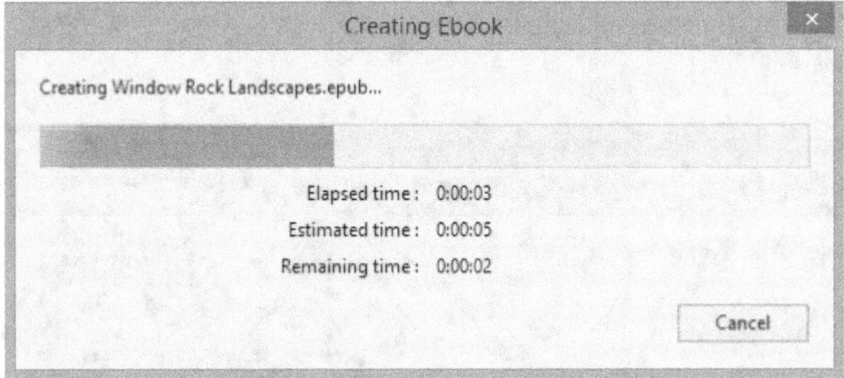

Figure 157. Creating Ebook.

When the Ebook is created, you will see the epub file in the Documents/Jutoh Documents folder. (Fig 158)

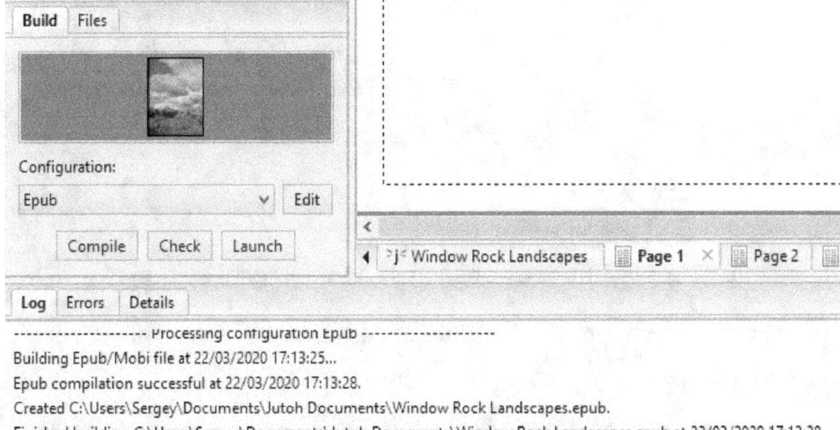

Figure 158. The EPUB file is created.

Now you can open Adobe Digital Editions, add the book to the library and view it. (Fig. 159)

Figure 159. Fixed layout book opened in Adobe Digital Editions.

Try to click each chapter in the table of contents and see if the correct page is displayed.

If your text font is too small or too big, you can change it in your EPUB book in Jutoh. Right click on the text object and select edit text. (Fig. 160)

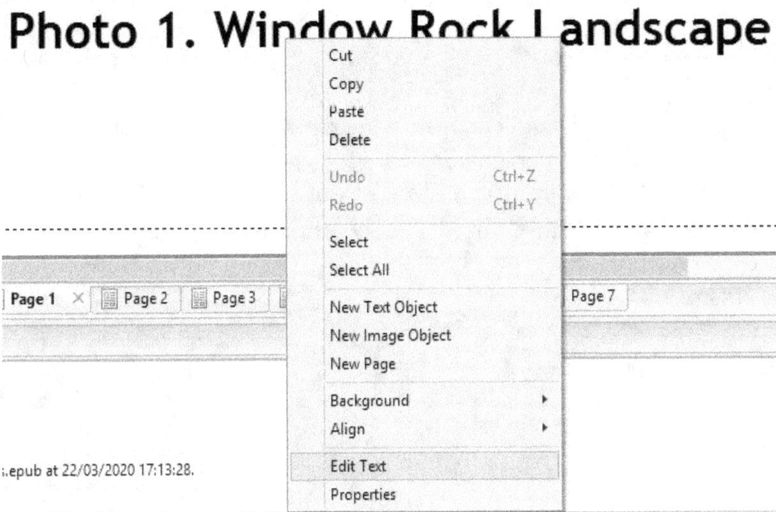

Figure 160. Edit text in the text object.

On the palette, select a Styles tab and change the text style. (Fig. 161)

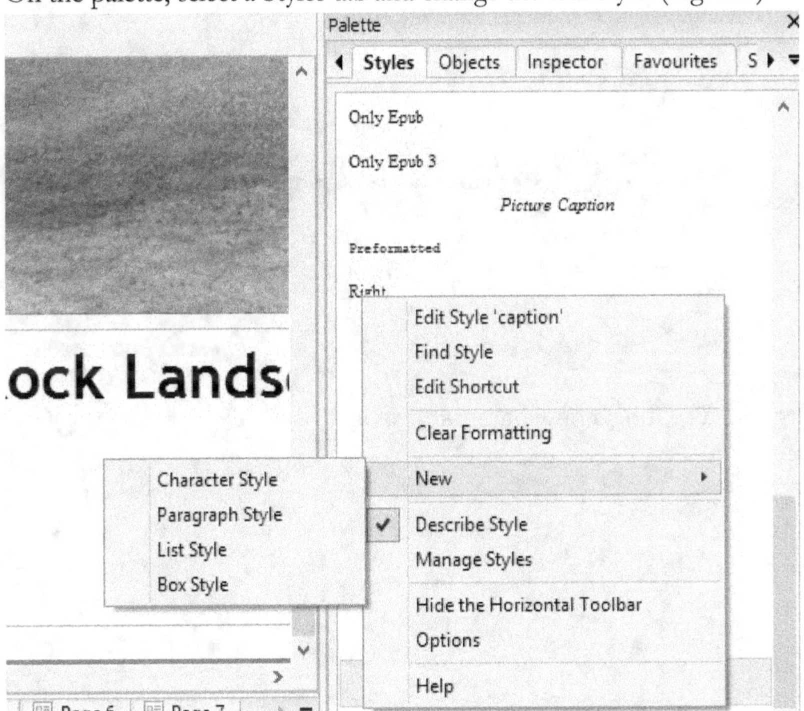

Figure 161. Change the text style.

Select the Paragraph style and enter the paragraph style name. You can use this style later for all your paragraphs.
You can enter CSS script or just copy style from exiting styles. I copied style from Heading 1 because I needed a big font size. (Fig. 162)

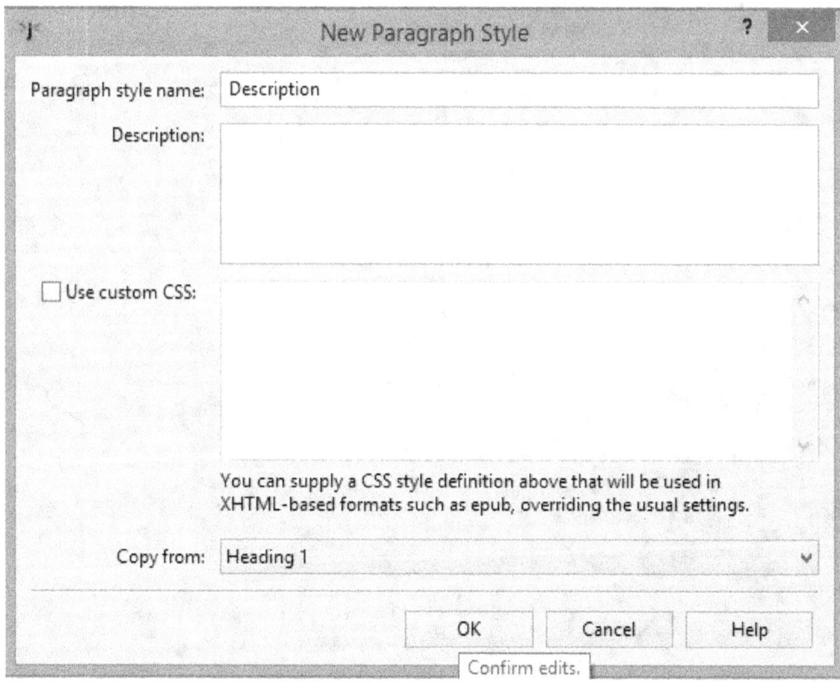

Figure 162. Creating a new paragraph style.

In the Font tab, select a font name and font size for your paragraph. (Fig. 163)

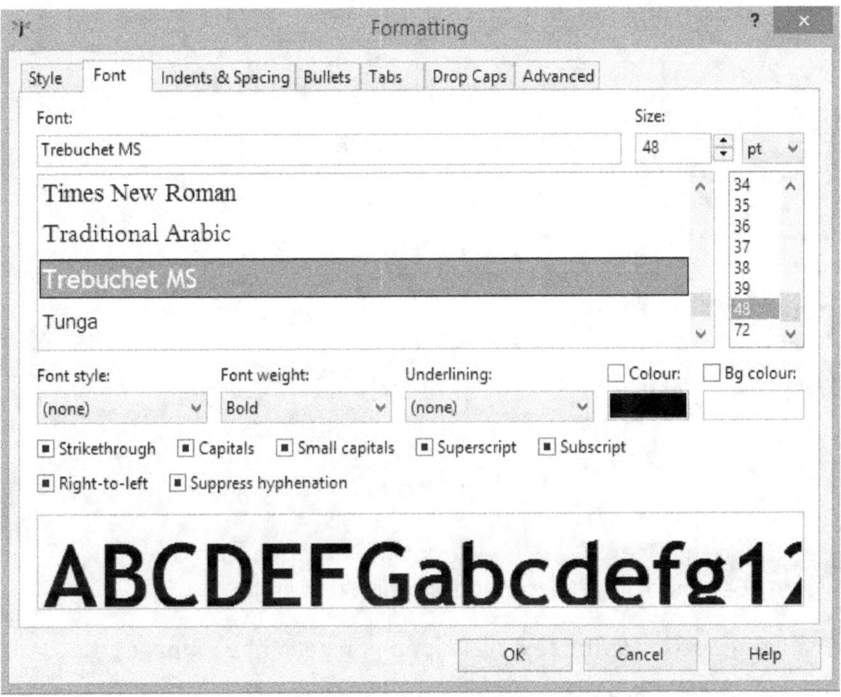

Figure 163. Selecting font name and size.

To change the style of your paragraph under the picture, select the style you just created. It was Description.

As soon, as you select it, the text style will be changed. (Fig. 164)

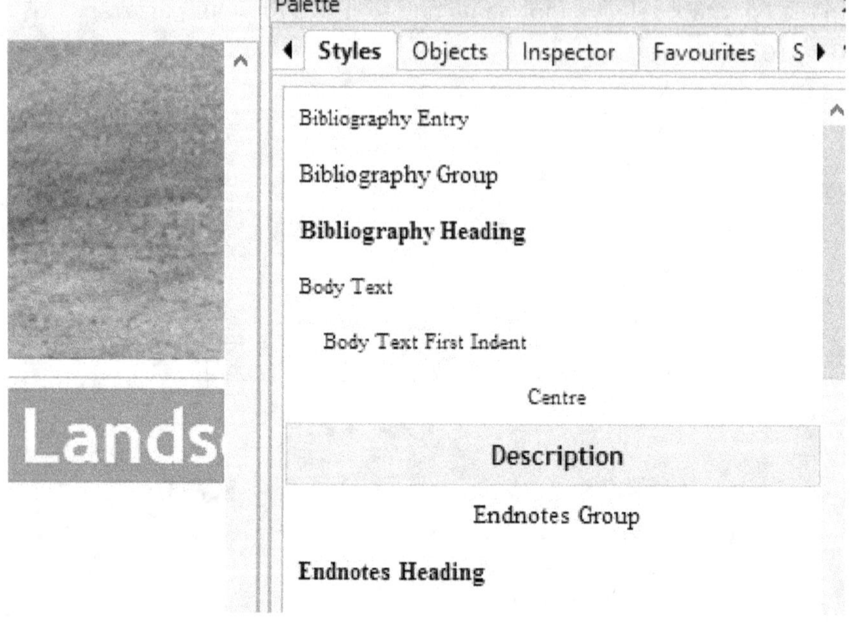

Figure 164. Changing a picture description text style.

Change the style for the text description on each of your pages. And recreate the book. Select Compile.

To create a Mobipocket book for Amazon Kindle, select mobi file under the configuration label and click the Compile button. (Fig. 165)

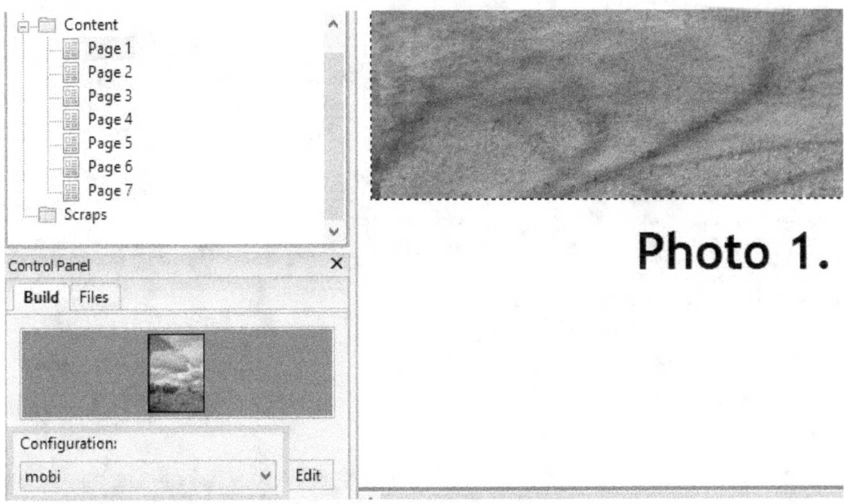

Figure 165. Select mobi file.

The mobi file will be created. (Figs. 166 and 167)

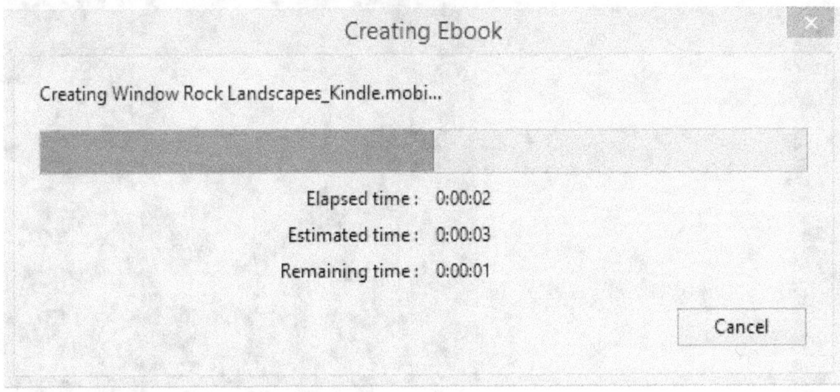

Figure 166. The mobi file creation.

The mobi file is created in the Documents/Jutoh Documents folder. (Fig. 167)

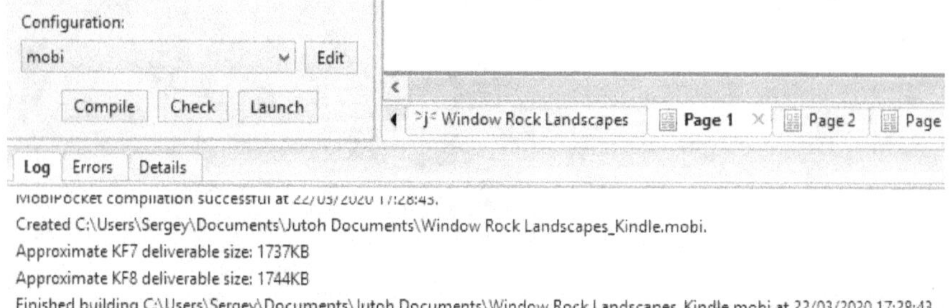

Figure 167. The mobi file is created.

Start Kindle for PC and add your mobi file to the Kindle library. The book is displayed in Kindle. (Fig.168)

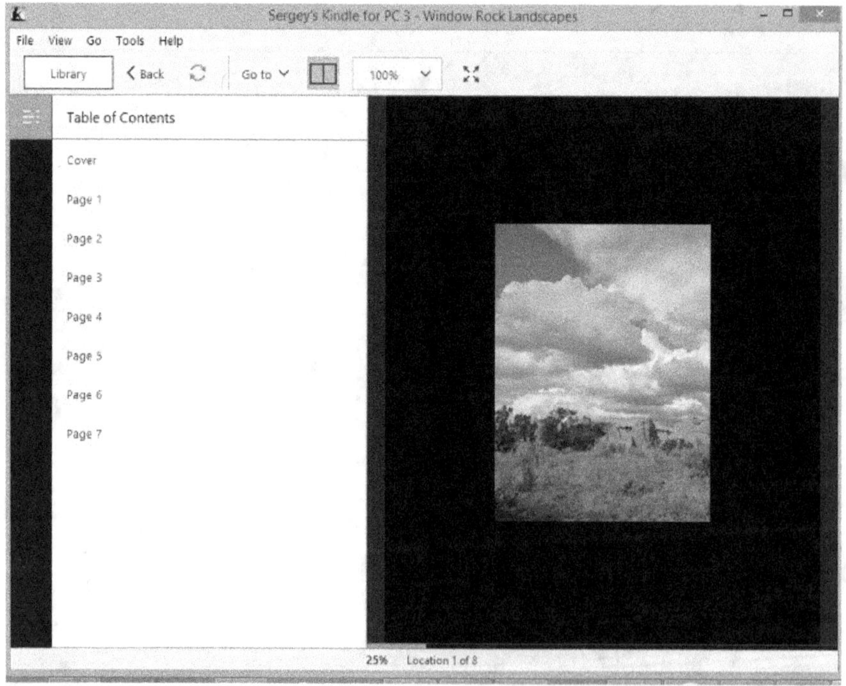

Figure 168. The book is displayed in Kindle

Try to click each option in the table of contents to make sure that the correct page is displayed. (Fig. 169)

Figure 169. The Mobi ebook is viewed in the Amazon Kindle for PC.

11.3. Print On Demand Formatting

Before creating a print on demand book, I would recommend installing LibreOffice open source suite for word processing. Jutoh recommends using it instead of MS Word. You can download it for free from https://www.libreoffice.org/download/download/

To create a print on demand book, start Jutoh and select a new project. In the first window enter your book metadata. (Fig. 170)

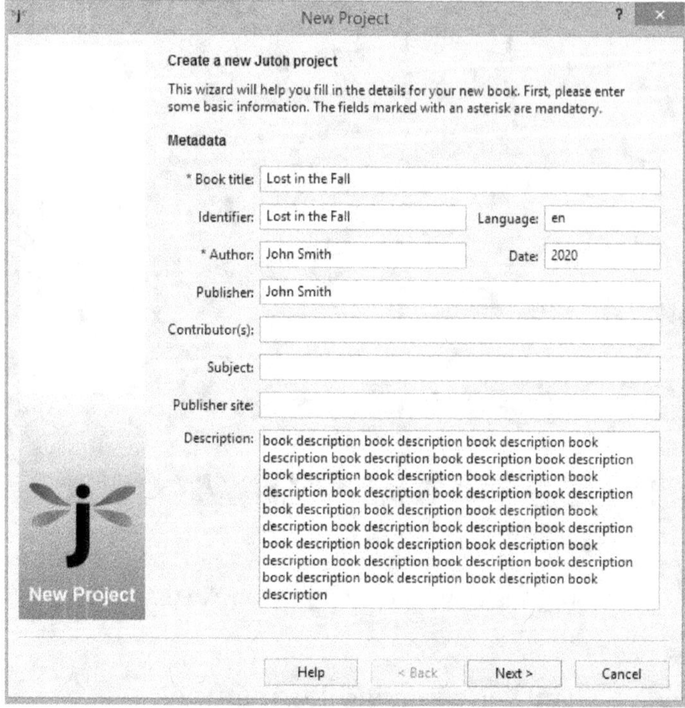

Figure 170. The meta data window.

Click the Next button.

In the next window select "Open Document" in the initial format list. (Fig. 171)

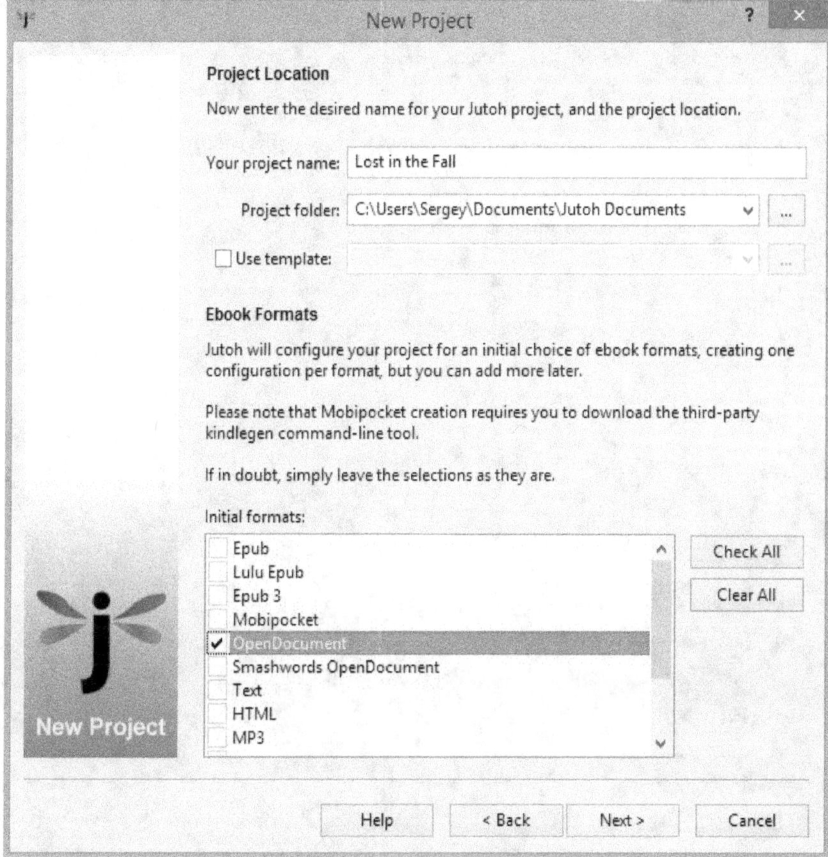

Figure 171. The Open Document format is selected.

Click the Next button.

In the next window, select Normal reflowable book. (Fig. 172)

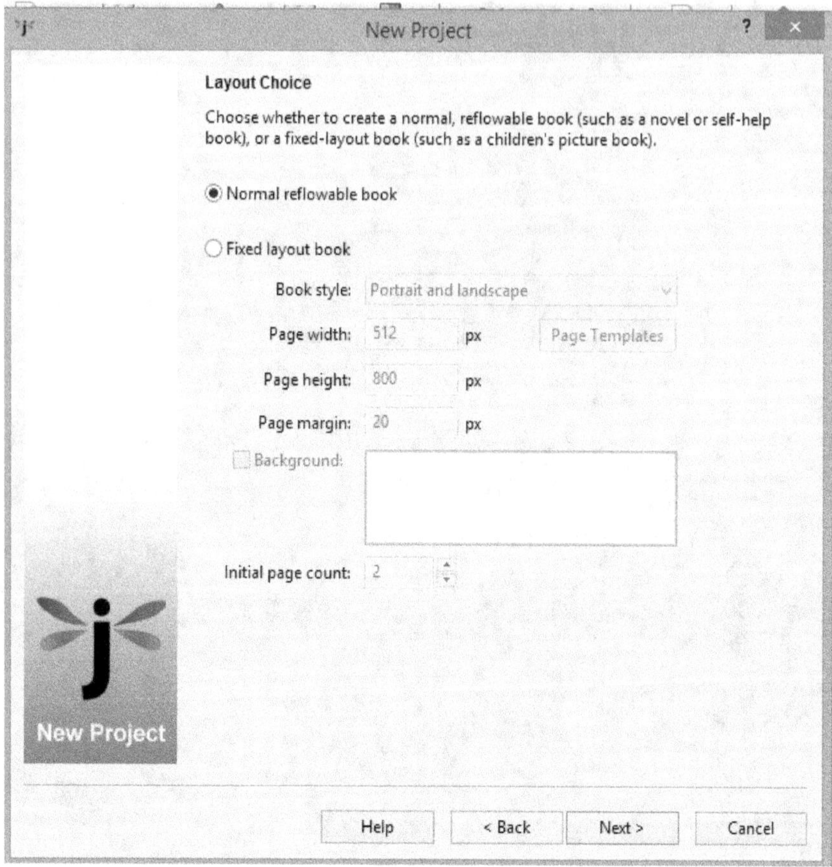

Figure 172. Normal reflowable book is selected.

Click the Next button.

In the next window, select Import images, if your book has images. My book has.

Mark the Resize images to max 800 pixels wide, otherwise, an image width may be bigger than the book page width. (Fig 173)

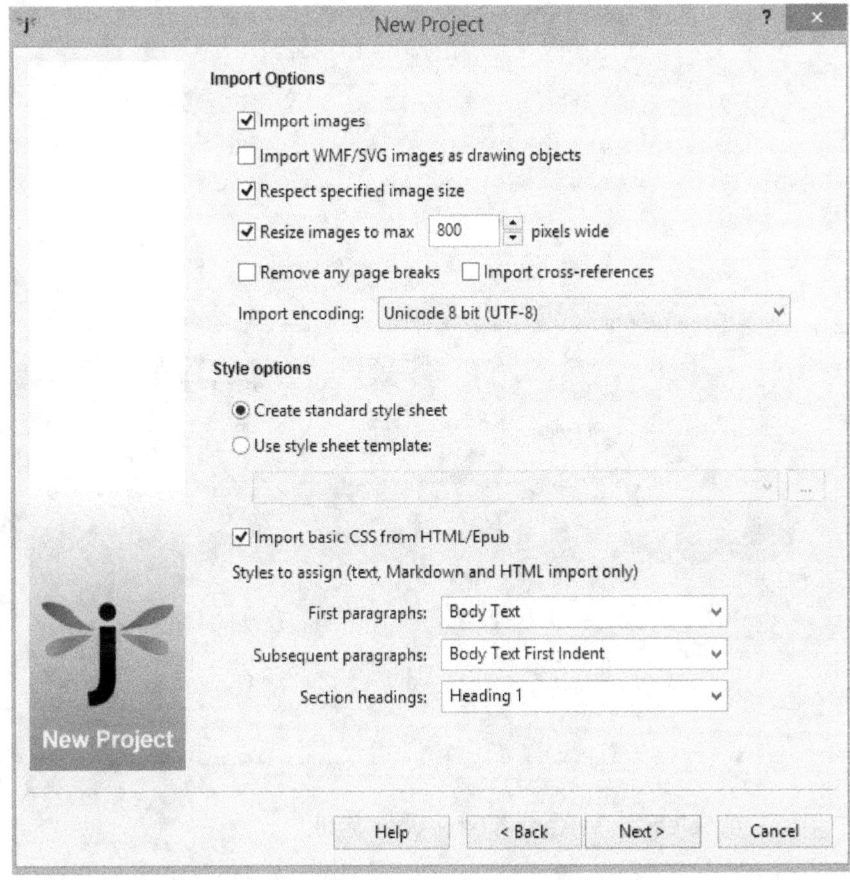

Figure 173. Import images.

Click the Next button. In the next window select your word document as a book file. (Fig. 174)

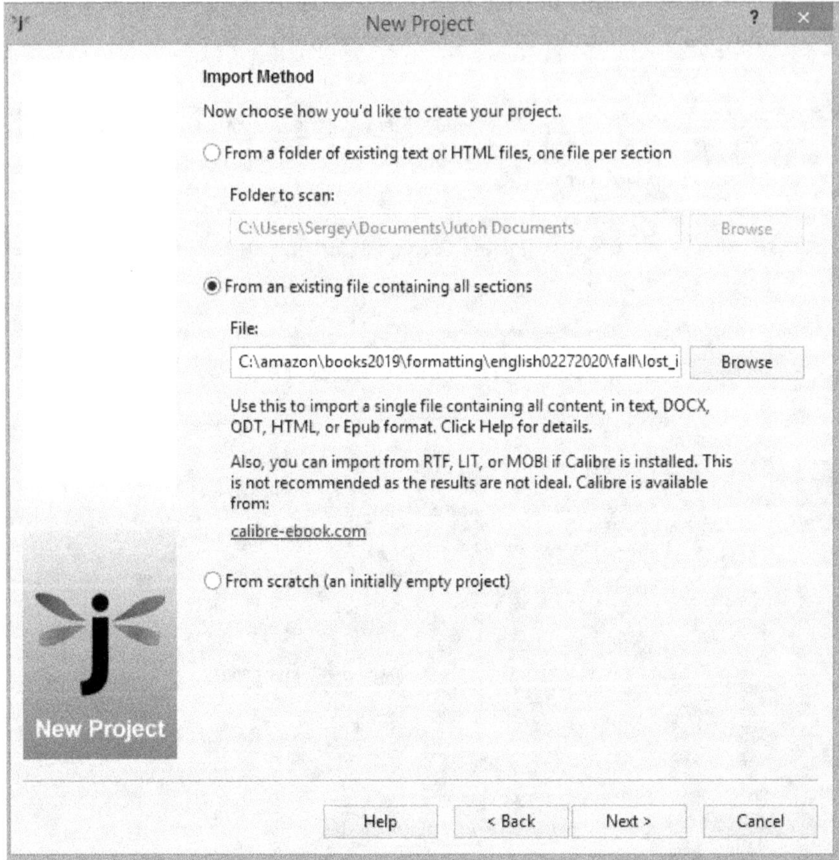

Figure 174. Select an existing file for your book.

Click the Next button. In the next window, select Split by style and select the style that you used for your chapter titles in your word document. You will see the chapter list in the Preview panel.

Mark the Remove unused styles from the stylesheet checkbox and Discard empty paragraphs checkbox.

The rest of the settings are is not important. (Fig. 175)

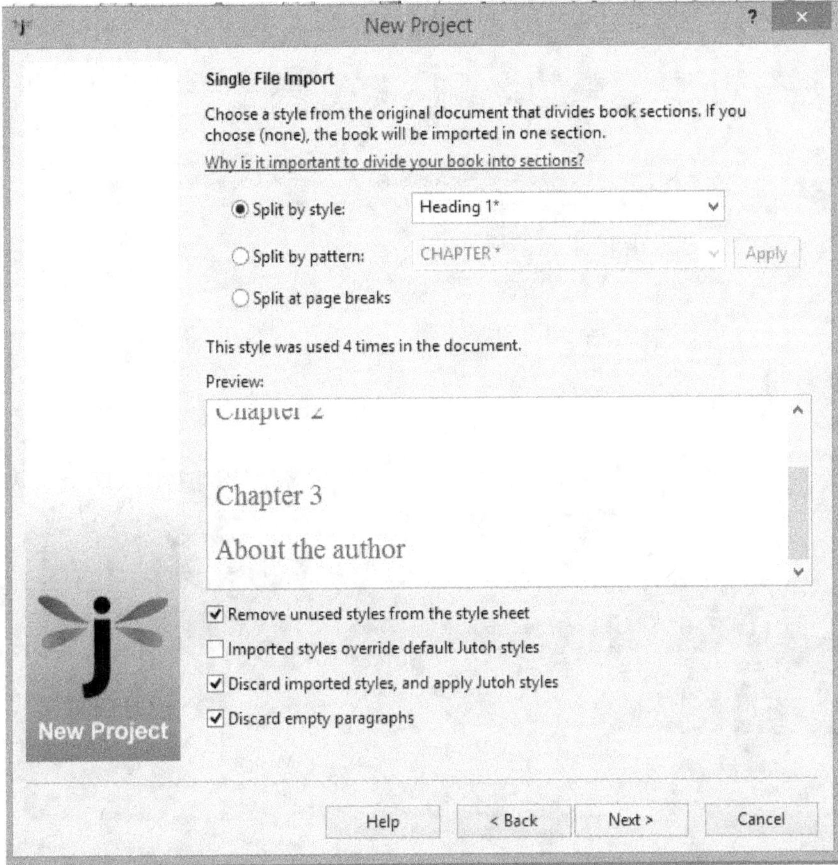

Figure 175. Split by style.

Click the Next button. In the next window select an existing file to add your cover.
Or you can skip this step since the paper book cover will be uploaded on the publisher website separately from the book content.

If you add the cover here you can always delete it later from your document. So, it does not matter. (Fig. 176)

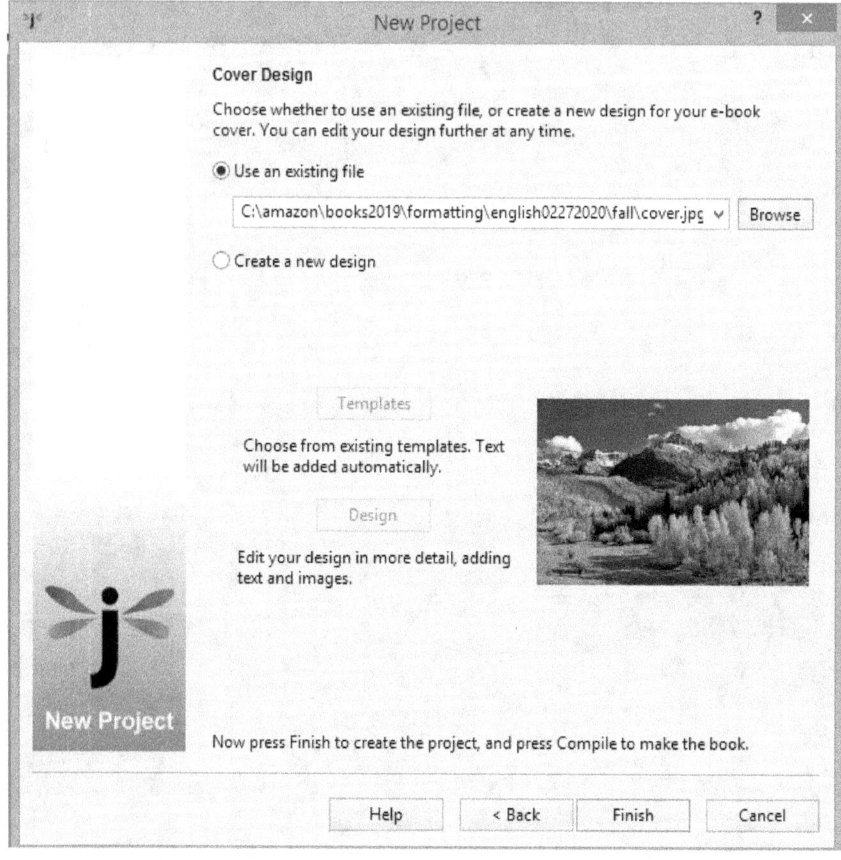

Figure 176. Add a cover.

Click the Next button.

The book project will be displayed. (Fig. 177)

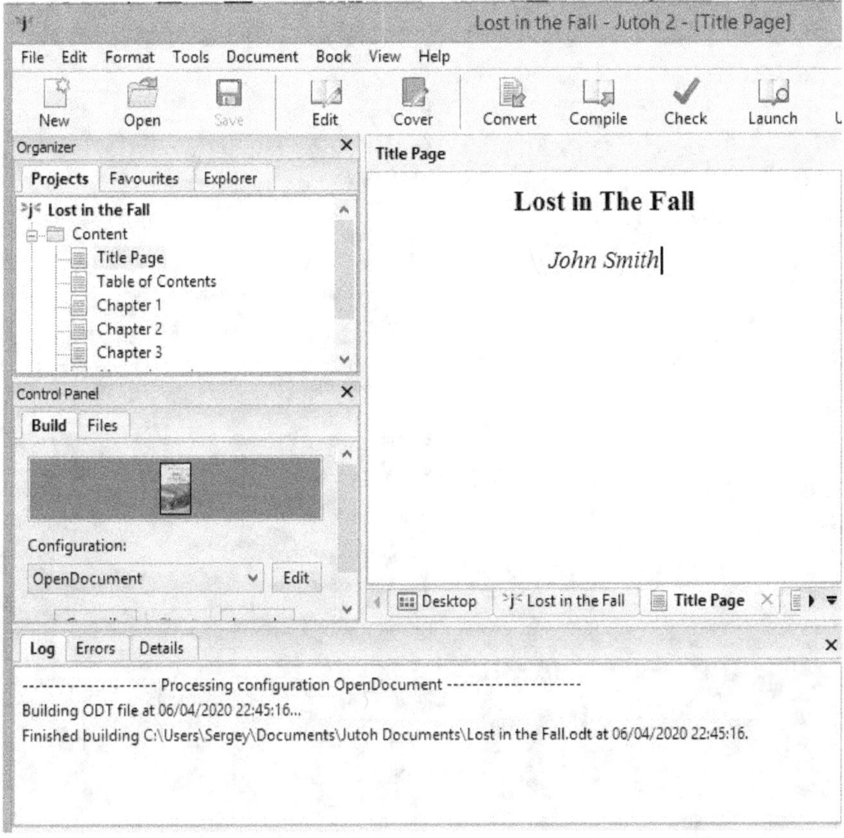

Figure 177. The book project is created.

Now you must add a table of contents. From the main menu, select
Book, Help with Print on Demand.(Fig. 178)

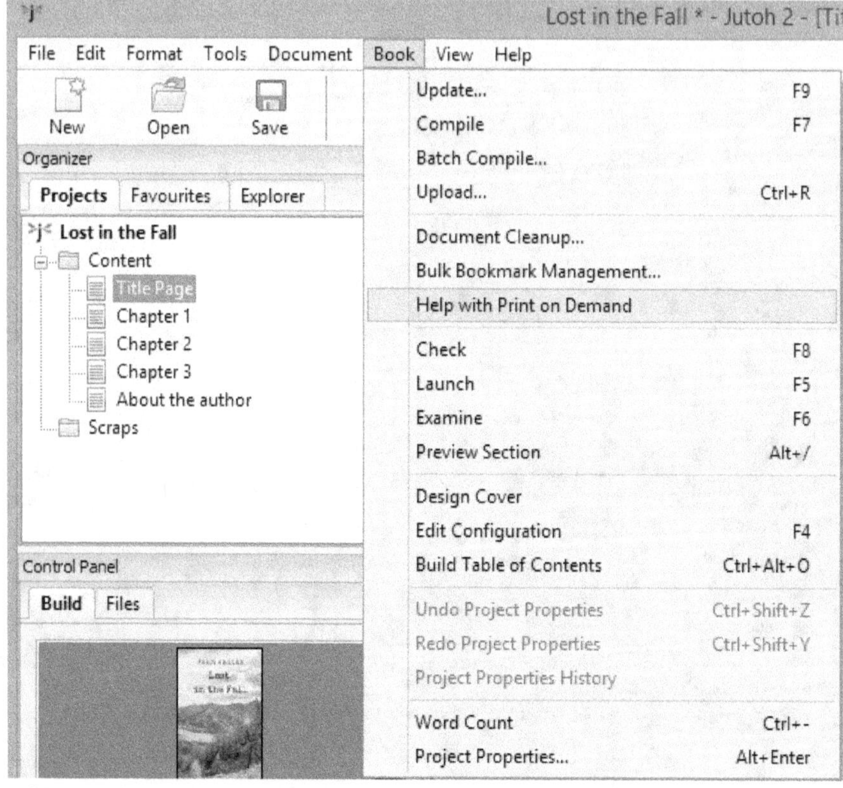

Figure 178. Help with Print on Demand.

Click the Next button. In the next window select OpenDocument in the
configuration drop down list.

If you do not have Libre Office installed on your PC, then mark the Use Microsoft Word checkbox. Otherwise do not mark any checkboxes. Click the Next button. (Fig. 179)

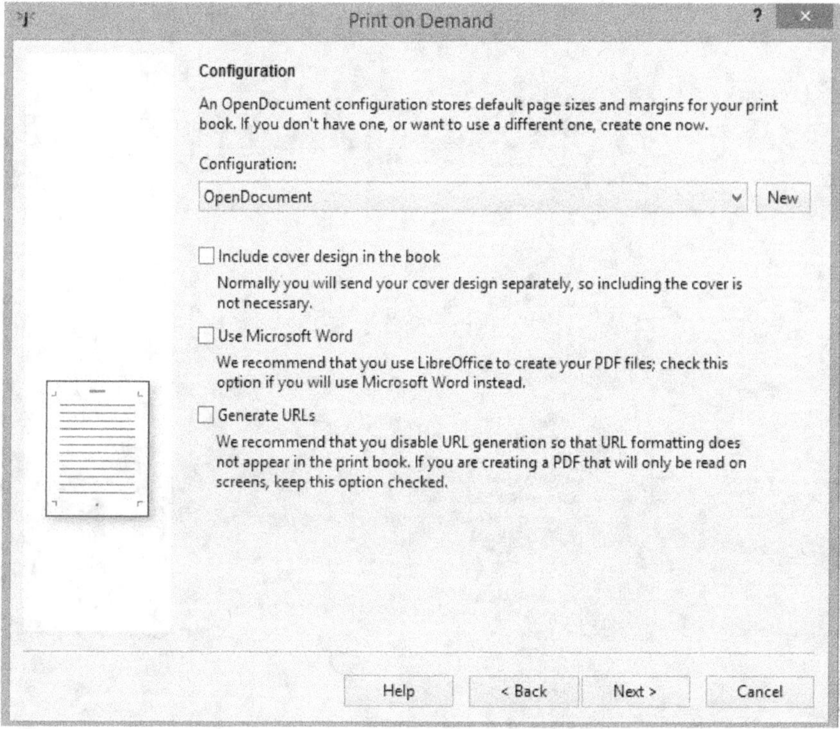

Figure 179. Configuration.

In the next window select a book page size and margins. (Fig. 180)

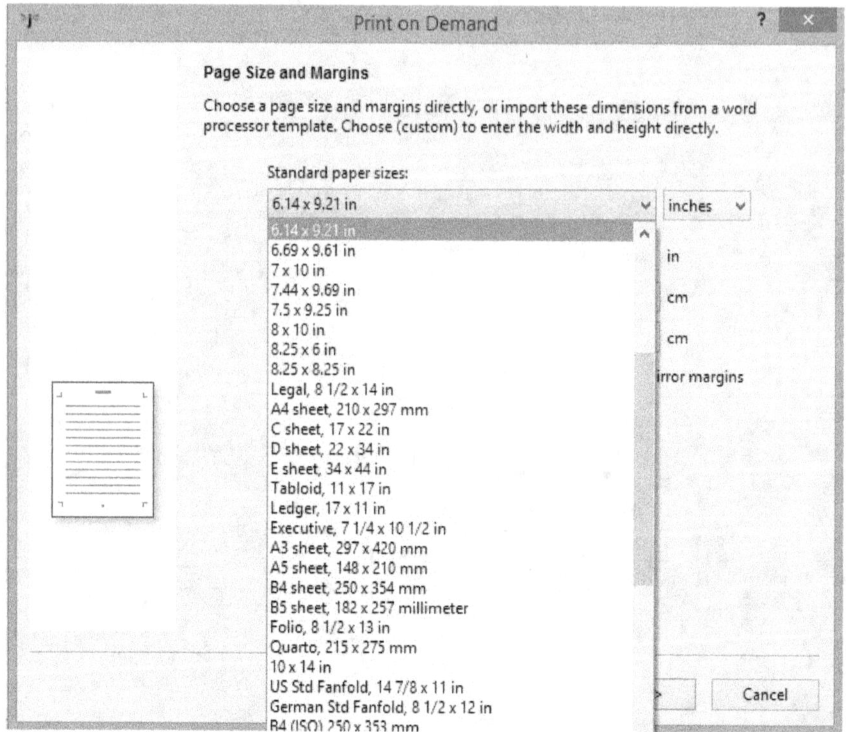

Figure 180. Book page size and margins.

Click the Next button. In the next window, I used the default setting.
(Fig. 181)

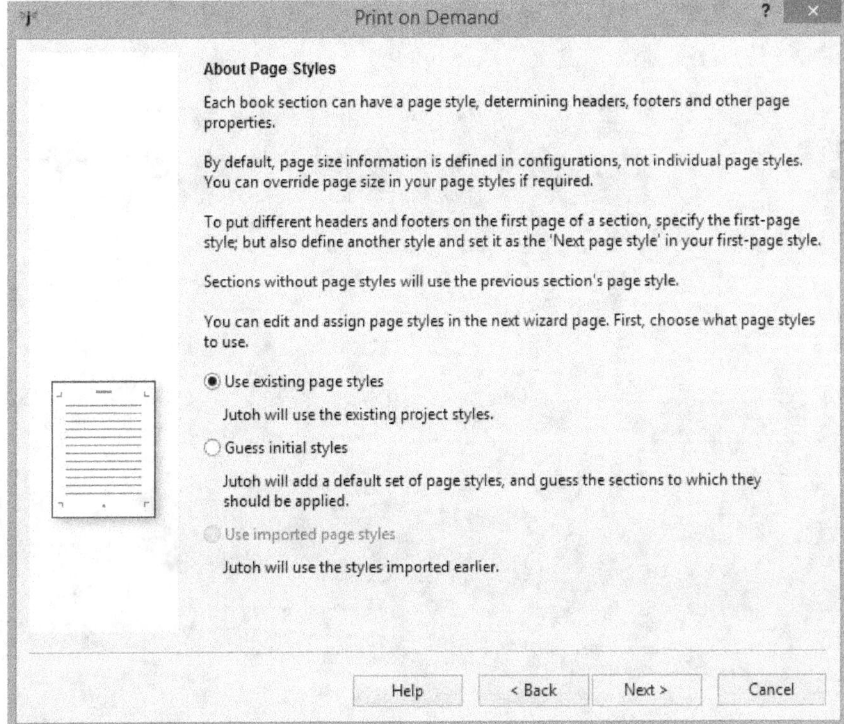

Figure 181. About page styles.

Click the Next button. In the next window, I accepted the default setting. (Fig. 182)

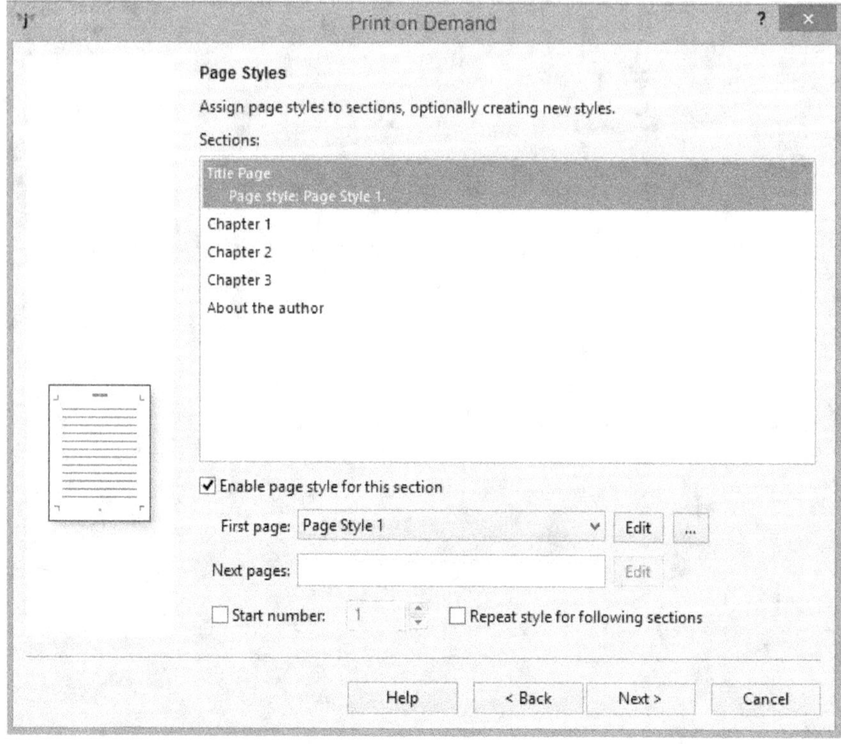

Figure 182. Page styles. Click the Next button.

In the next window, you can edit Header and Footer styles. (Fig. 183)

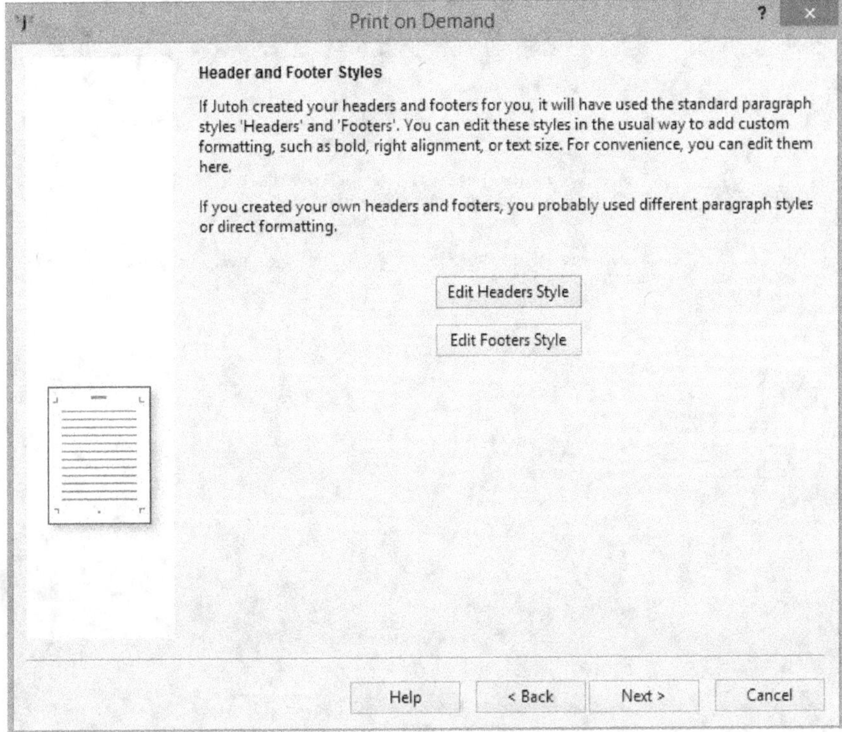

Figure 183. Edit Header and Footer style.

Click the Next button.

In the next window, you can edit the document outline style. I accepted the default setting.(Fig. 184)

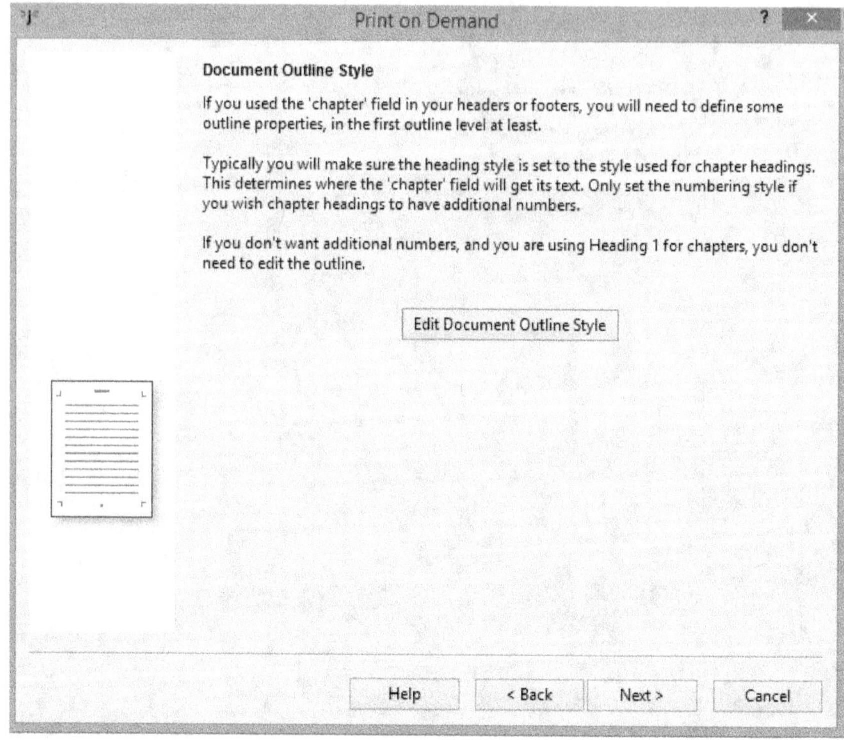

Figure 184. Edit document outline style.

If you click the Edit Document Outline Style, you will see the following window. Here you can select a style for each outline level. For example, for Level 1 you can select Heading 1, for Level 2 – Heading 2 and so on. (Fig. 185)

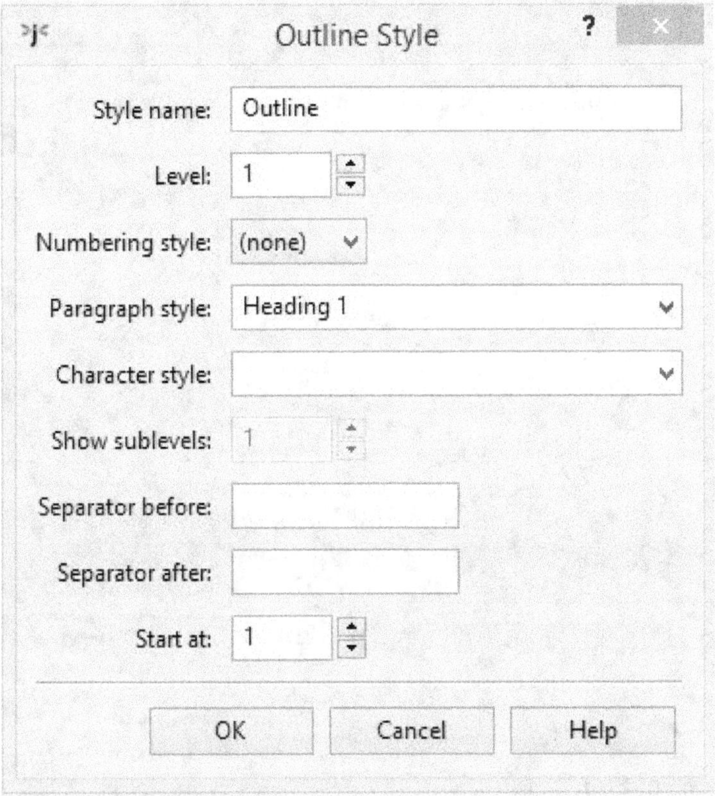

Figure 185. Outline Style.

Click the Next button. In the next window click the Compile button.
 (Fig. 186)

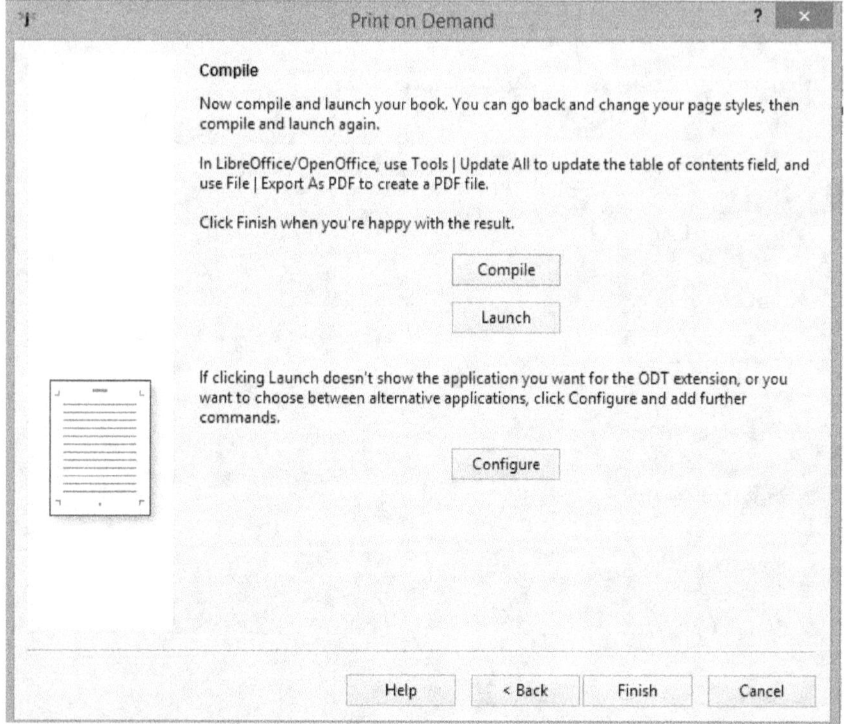

Figure 186. Compile.

Click the Finish button.

To create a table of contents, in the main menu, select Book, Build Table of Contents. (Fig. 187)

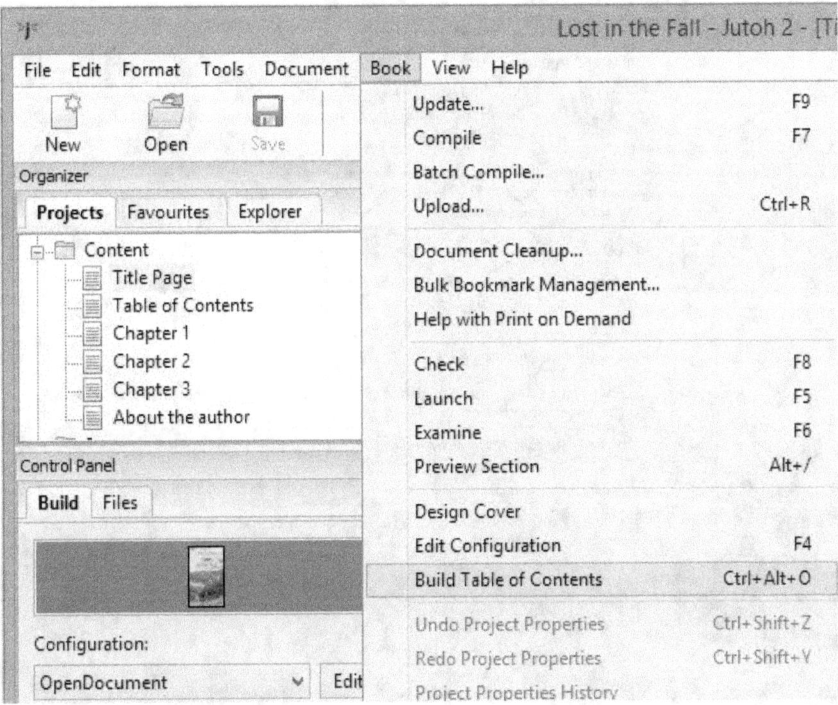

Figure 187. Build Table of Contents.

In the next window mark the checkbox "Create Contents with Jutoh's help" and checkbox "Create a contents page".(Fig. 188)

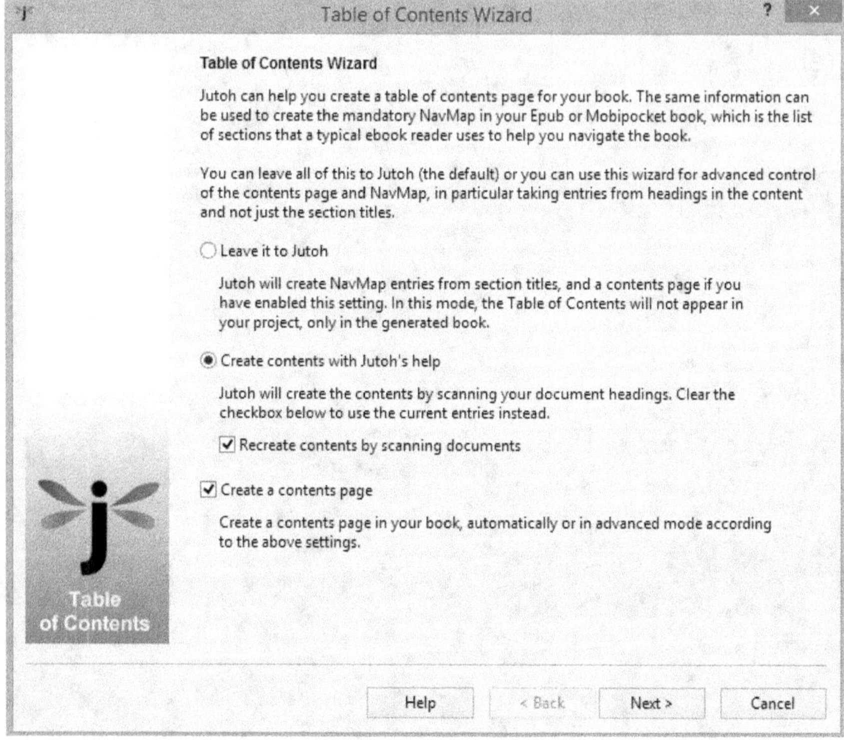

Figure 188. Create Contents with Jutoh's help.

Click the Next button.

The "Jutoh could not find a suitable table of contents section. Insert a new table of contents document?" message is displayed. Click the Yes button. (Fig. 189)

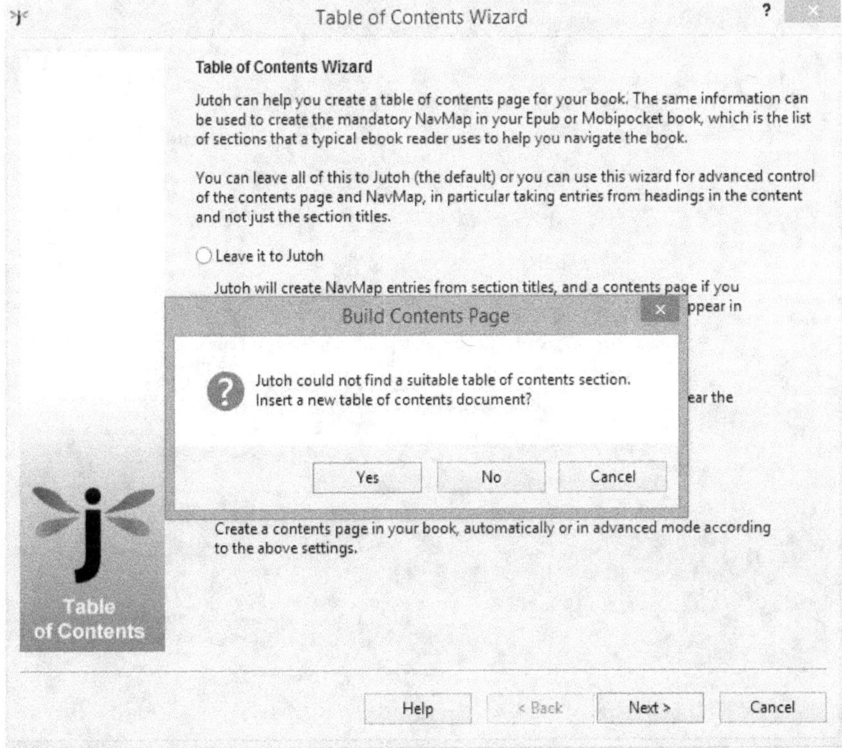

Figure 189. Insert a new table of contents document?

Click the Next button.

In the next window, select the Max heading level. I have only one level. My book has chapters but no subchapters. Since it is a paper book, you don't need a URL link style. I selected Comment Text for the Link style.
I did not change any other setting here. (Fig. 190)

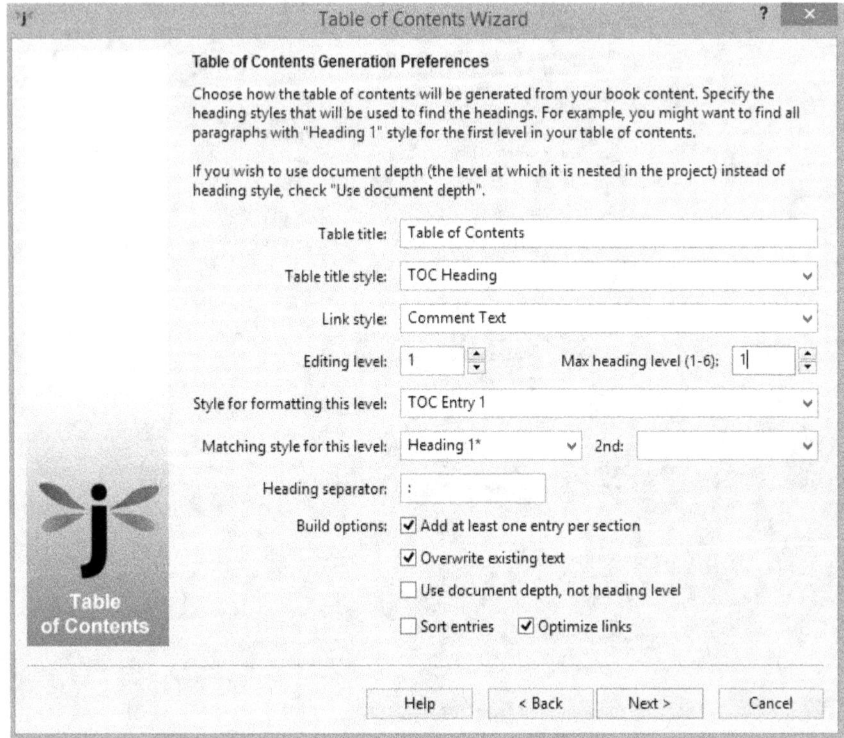

Figure 190. Table of Contents General Preferences.

Click the Next button.

In the next window you can move table of contents to the end of the book. To achieve that click the arrow button. (Fig. 191)

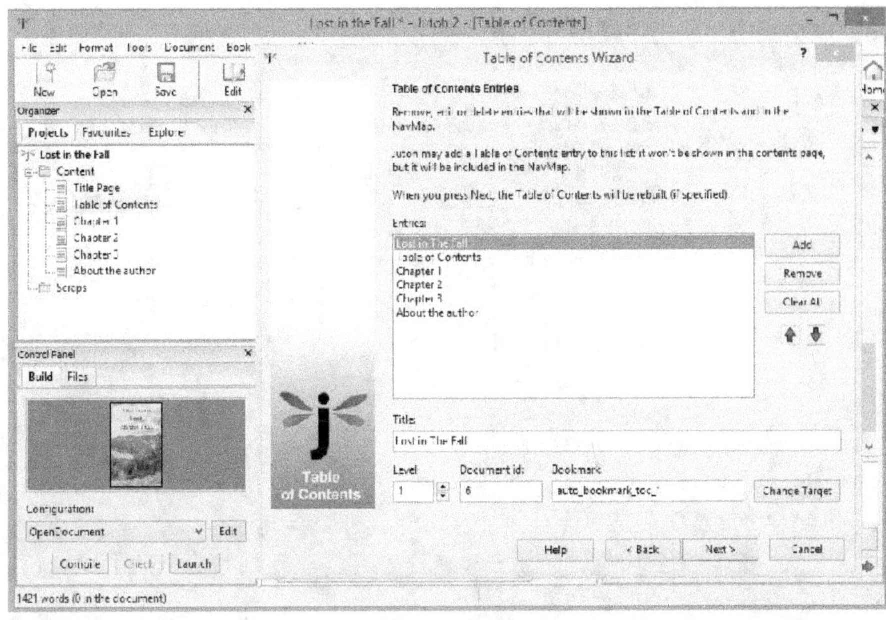

Figure 191. Table of Contents Wizard.

Click the Next button. The Finished window is displayed. (Fig. 192)

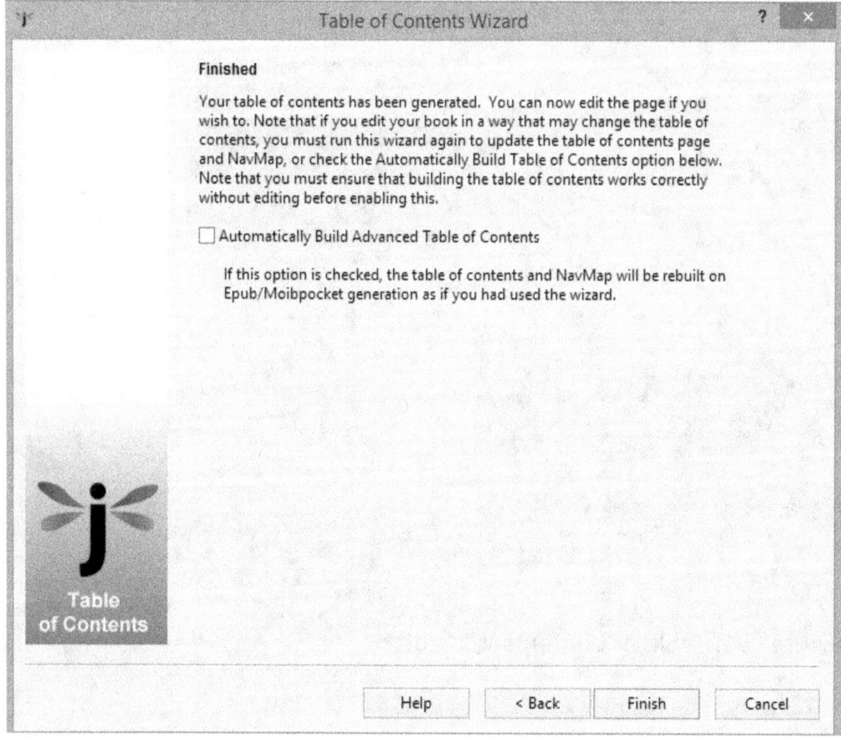

Figure 192. Finished.

Click the Finish button. The table of contents page is created. (Fig. 193)

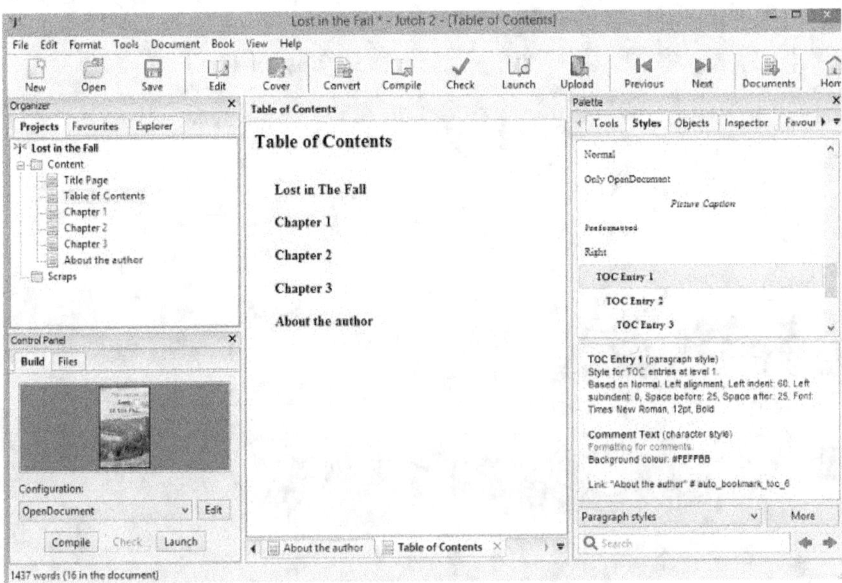

Figure 193. The table of contents page.

Click the Compile button. The ODT file is created. (Fig. 194)

Figure 194. The ODT file is created.

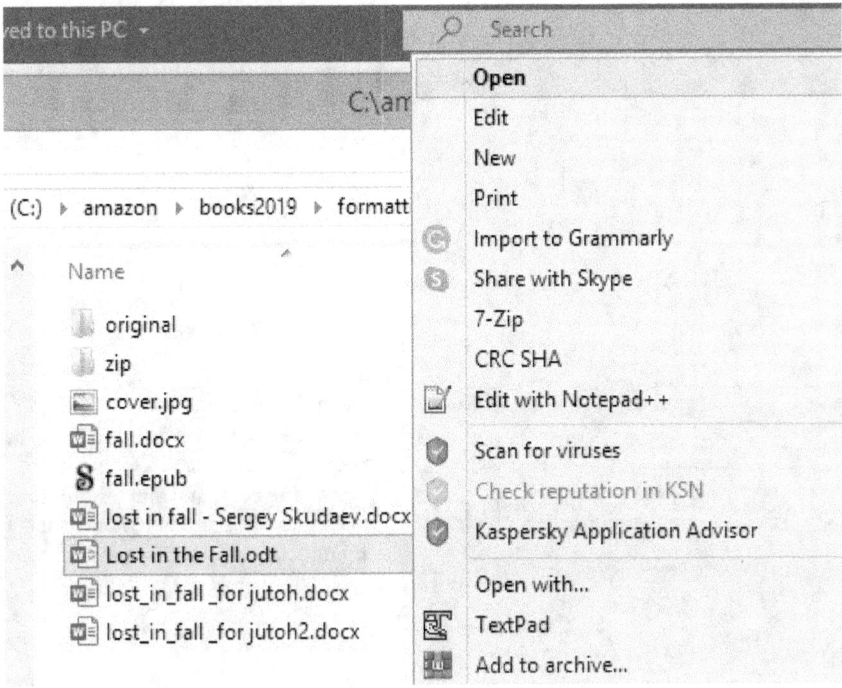

Figure 195. Open the .odt file in MS Word.

The document is opened in MS Word. You will see the table of contents page with the UPDATE ME text. (Fig. 196)

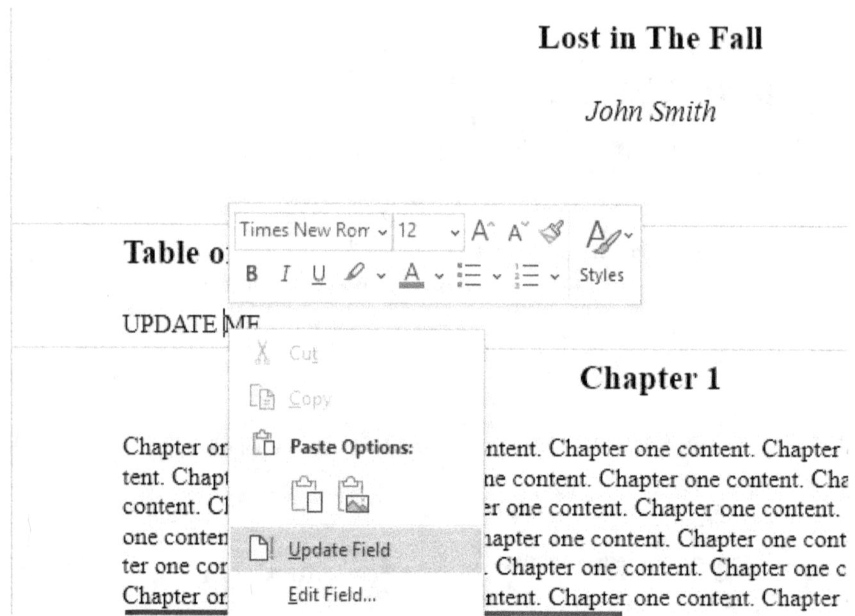

Figure 196. UPDATE ME

Right click on the UPDATE ME text and select Update field. The table of contents will be created. (Fig. 197)

Lost in The Fall

John Smith

Chapter 1

Chapter one content. Chap-

Figure 197. The created table of contents.

Save the word document. (Fig. 198).

Lost in The Fall

John Smith

Lost in The Fall ....

Chapter 1 ....

Chapter 2 ....

Chapter 3

Microsoft Word ☒

Want to save your changes to "Lost in the Fall.odt"?

If you click "Don't Save", a recent copy of this file will be temporarily available.
Learn more

Save   Don't Save   Cancel

Figure 198. Saving the word document.

You can try to open your odt file in both, MS Word and Libre Office and see what is more convenient for you.

Then you can save the document as a PDF in both applications and see which PDF is better. Good luck!

12. Appendix: Installing Software You will Need to Create Your E-Book

12.1. Installation of Gimp

Download the GIMP program here:

http://gimp.editor.ideaprog.download

Double-click the downloaded gimp-2.10.8-setup-2.exe file. Now, 2.10.8 is the latest version. When you download it, the version may change. Select your language as in Figure 199 and click OK.

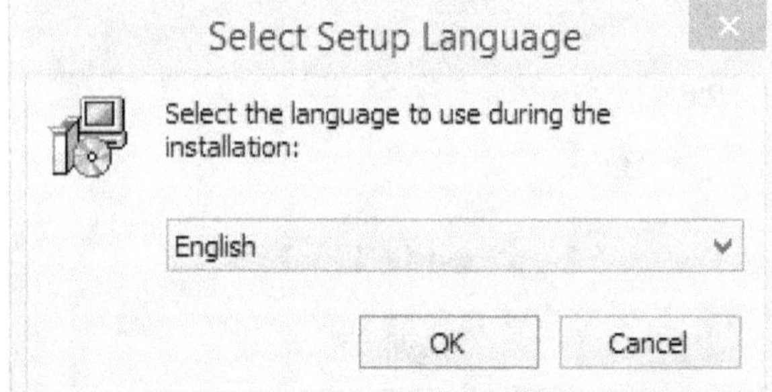

Figure 199. Selecting the language for installing GIMP. (Fig. 200)

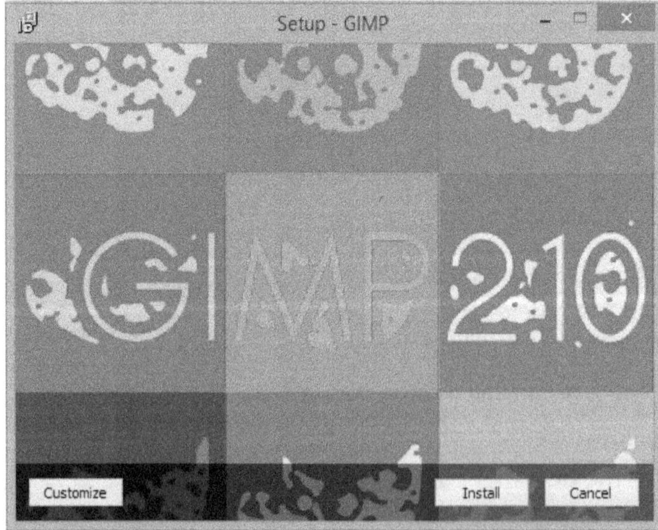

Figure 200. Installation has begun.

Click the Install button. The installation will start. (Fig 201)

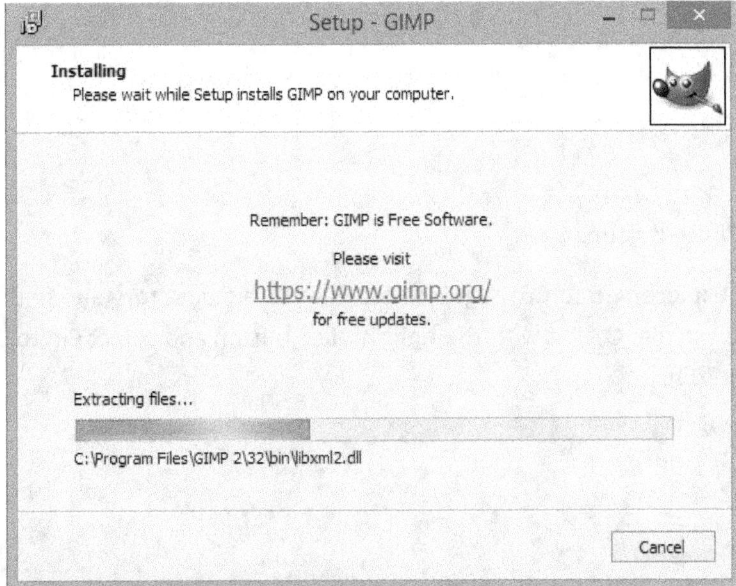

Figure 201. Installation of GIMP in progress

Figure 202. Installation of GIMP is completed.

Click the Finish button.

Open File Explorer, go to C:\Program Files\GIMP2\bin directory and find gimp-2.10.exe file. Click it with the right mouse button and select Pin to Start. (Fig. 203).

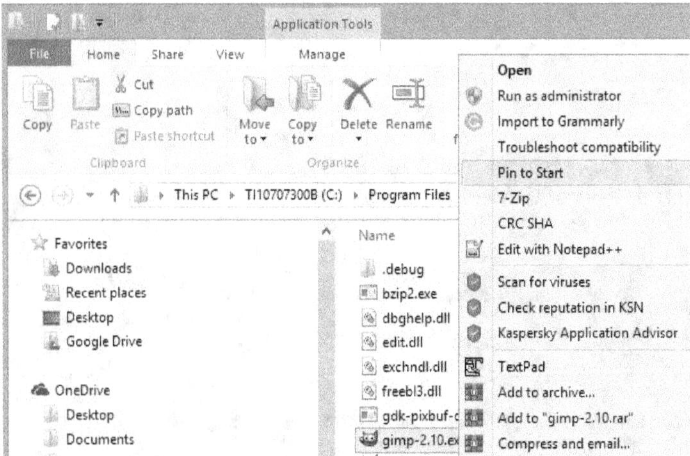

Figure 203 Pin to Start.

The GIMP application will be added to the start menu.

Click the gimp-2.10.exe file with the right mouse again and select Pin to Taskbar. (Fig. 204)

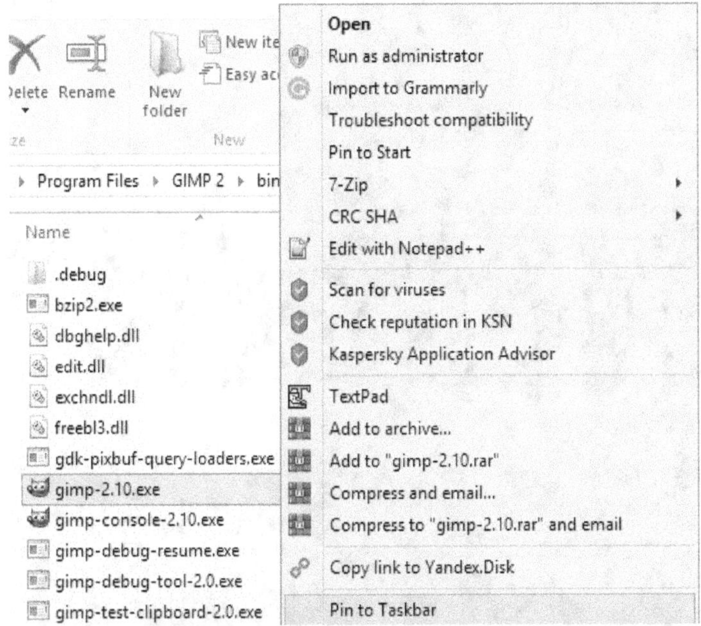

Figure 204. Pin to Taskbar.

The GIMP short cut icon will be added to the task bar. (Fig. 205)

Figure 205. A GIMP icon appears on the taskbar.

12.2. Installation of Calibre

Download calibre from http://calibre-ebook.com/
download_windows64. (Fig. 206)

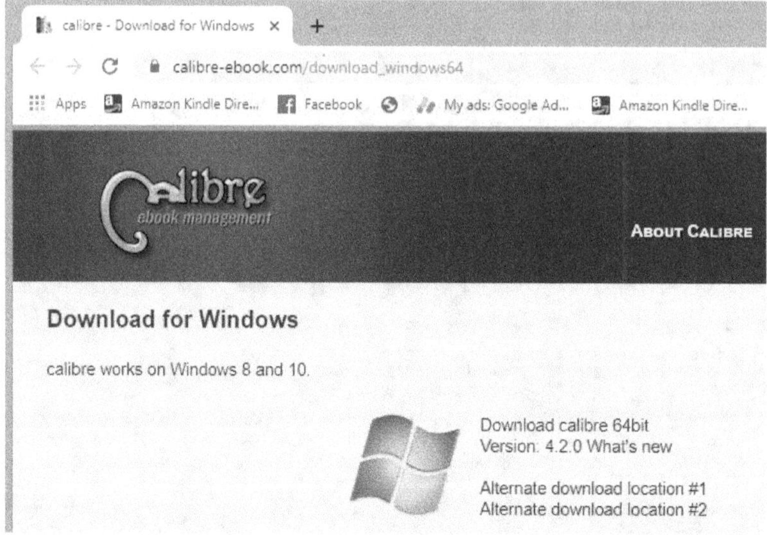

Figure 206. Download Calibre for Windows.

Find the downloaded calibre-64bit-4.8.0.msi file and double click it to start installation. When you download it, the version number may be different. The Welcome window will be displayed. (Fig. 207)

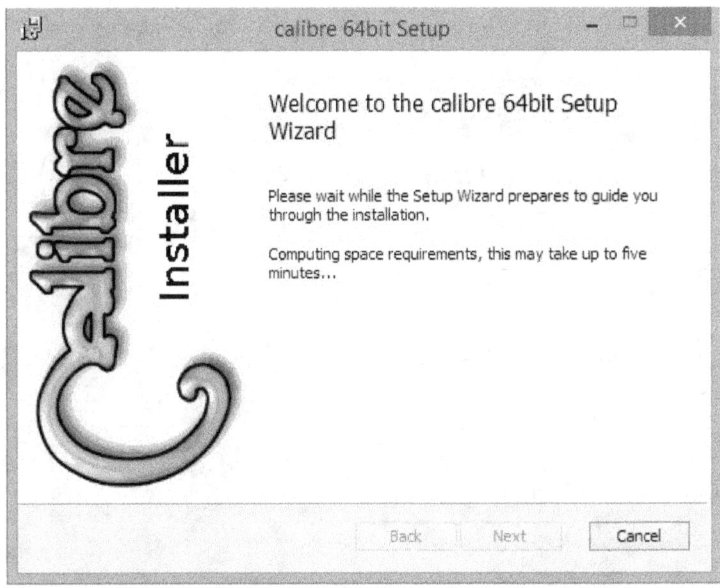

Figure 207. The Setup Wizard prepares the installation guide.

When the Next button becomes active, click it.

The calibre 64bit License Agreement window will be displayed. (Fig. 208)

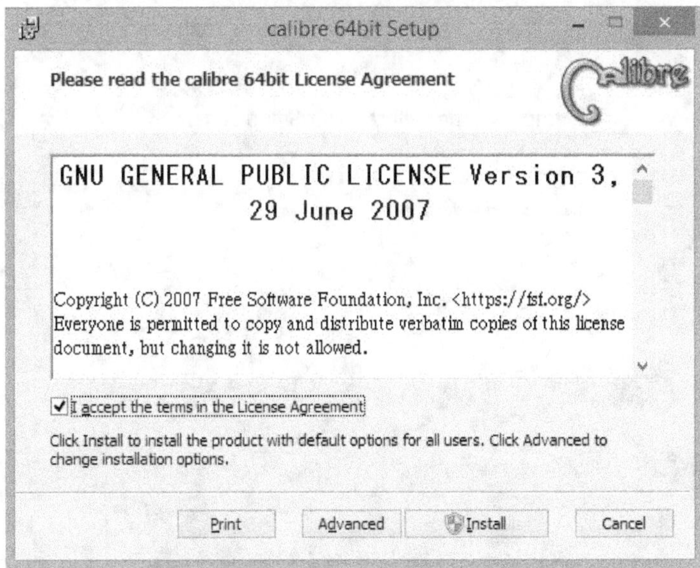

Figure 208. Accept the terms and click Install.

Mark "I accept the terms in the License Agreement" and click the Install button.

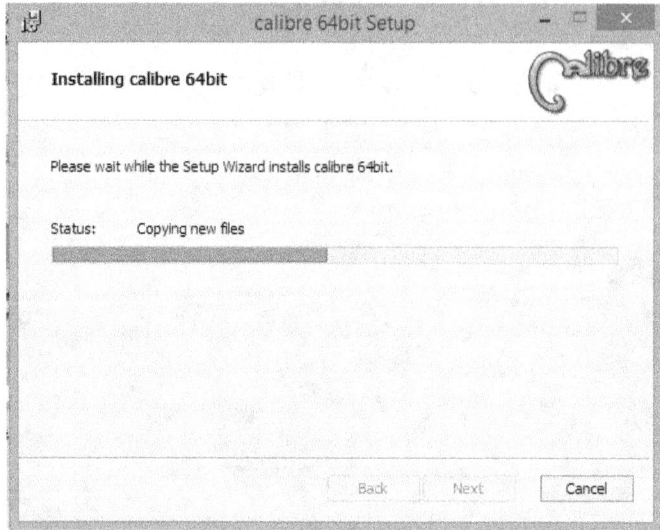

Figure 209 Installation started. When the Next button becomes active, click it.

The Completed the calibre 64bit Setup Wizard window will be displayed. (Fig. 210)

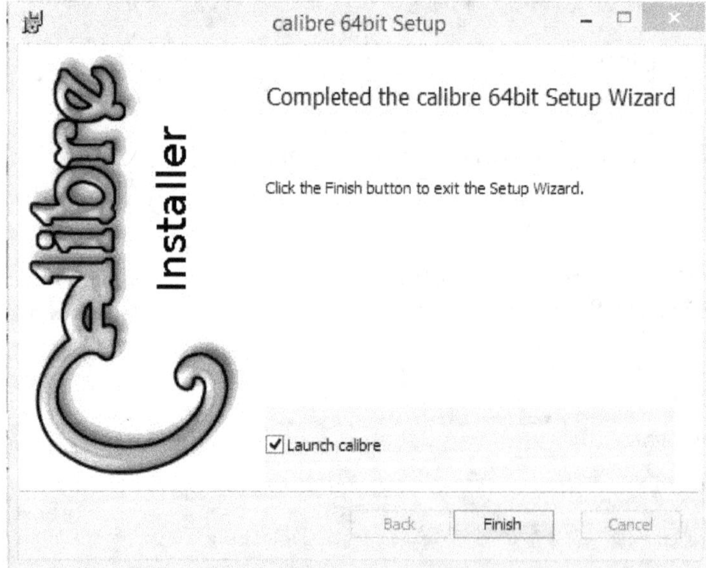

Figure 210. Installation is completed.

Click the Finish button. The software is installed.

12.3. Installation of Sigil

Find in the Google Sigil Download link. You may use https://www.techspot.com

Select Window 64-bit for the Windows PC or macOS for Mac. (Fig. 211)

Figure 211. Download the Sigil application.

The License Agreement window will be displayed. (Fig. 212)

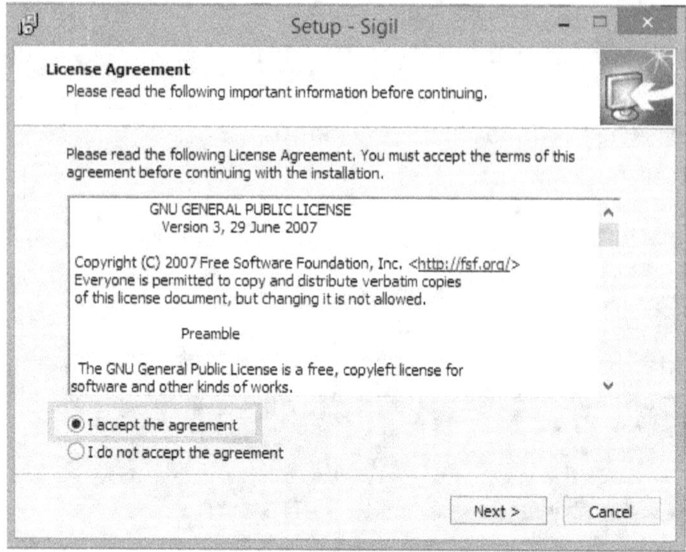

Figure 212. Accept the agreement. Click Next

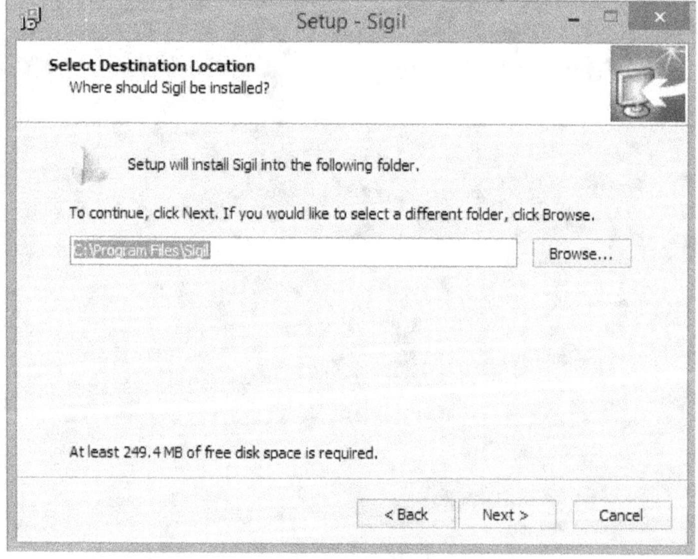

Figure 213. Accept the default path and click Next.

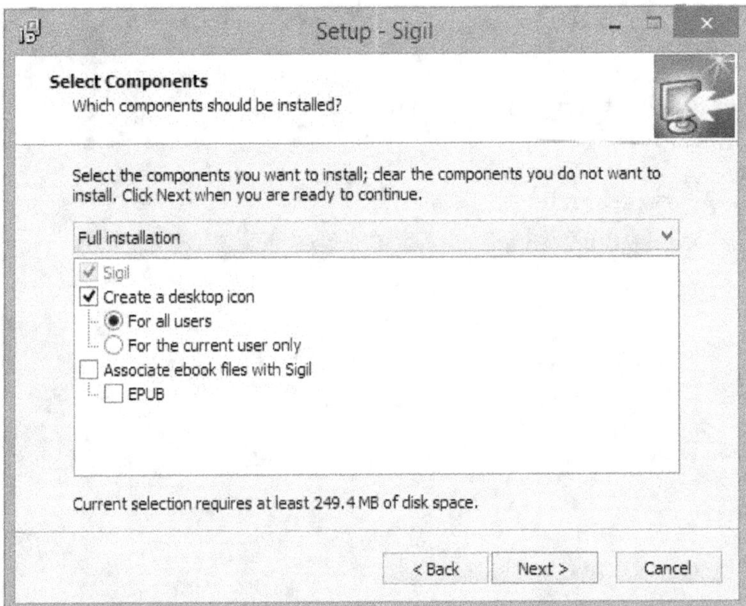

Figure 214. Select the Create a desktop icon, "For all users" and click Next.

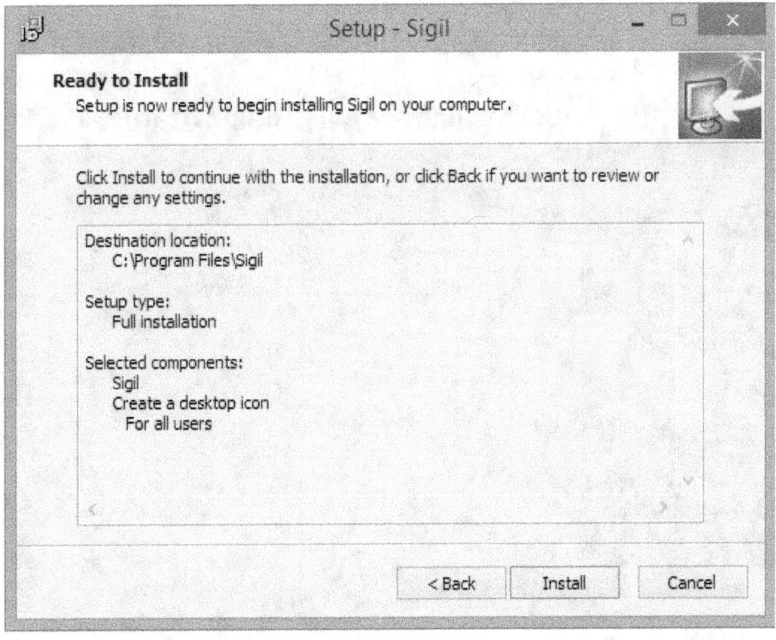

Figure 215. Click the Install button.

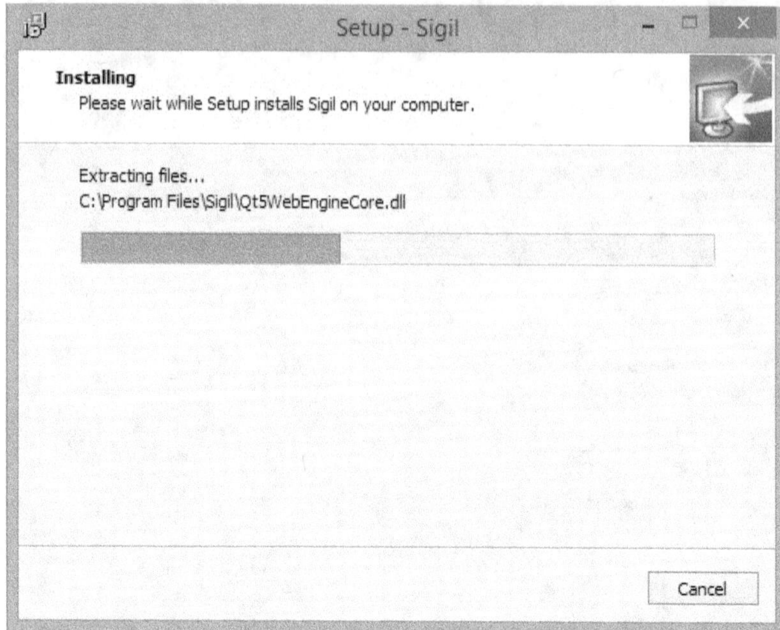

Figure 216. Installation in progress.

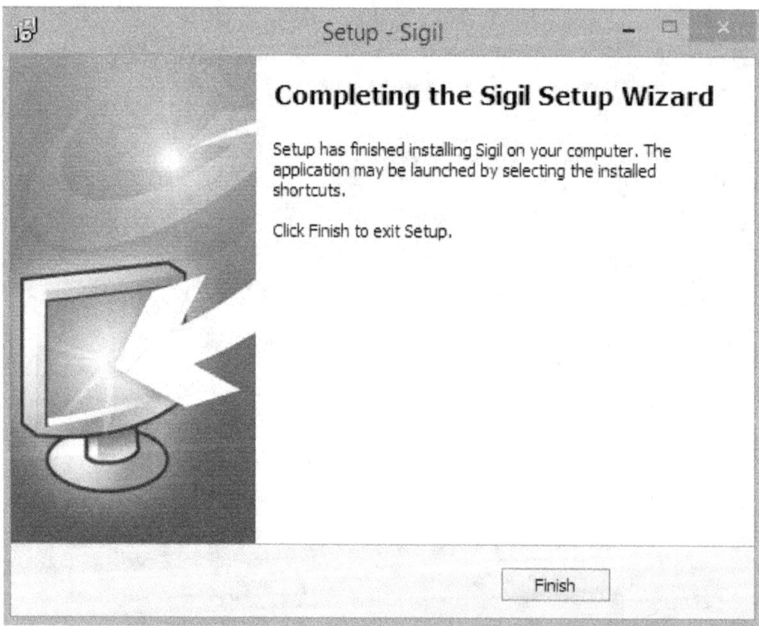

Figure 217. Installation is completed. Click the Finish button.

12.4. Installation of Adobe Digital Edition

Download Adobe Digital Edition from here:

https://www.adobe.com/solutions/ebook/digital-editions/download.html.

Figure 218. Download Adobe Digital Edition.

Find the ADE_4.5_Installer.exe file and double click it. The installation starts.

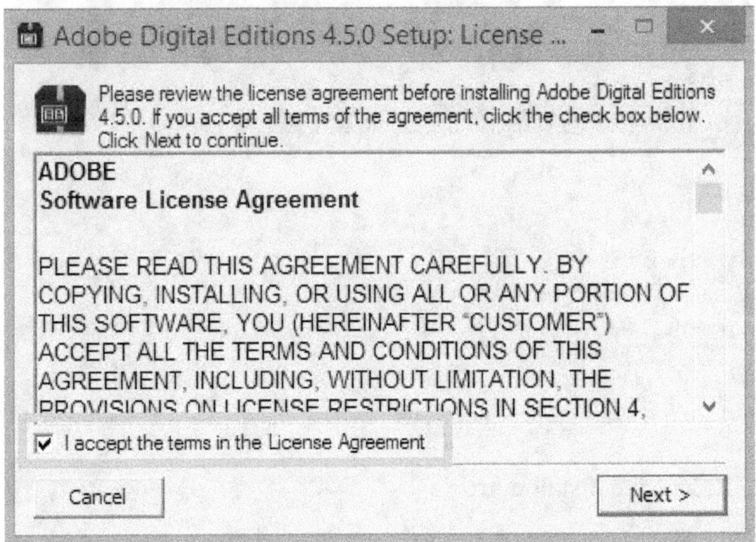

Figure 219. Installation of Adobe Digital Edition. Accept the terms and click Next.

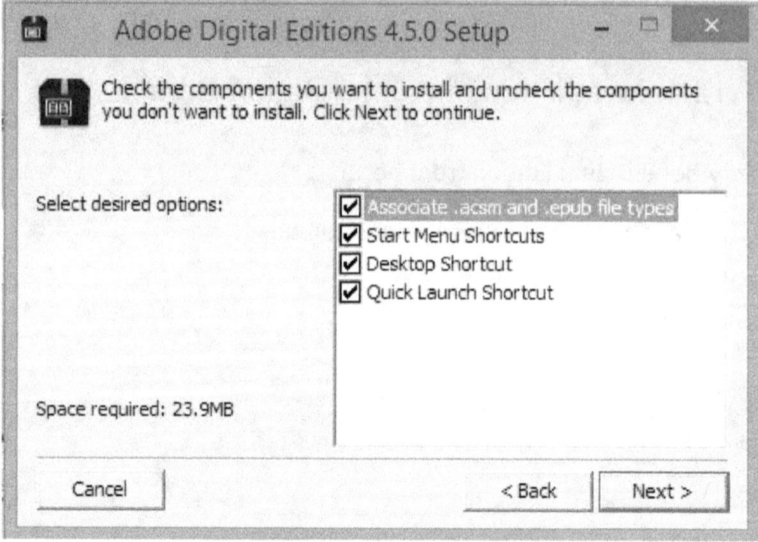

Figure 220. Accept the Default setting and click Next

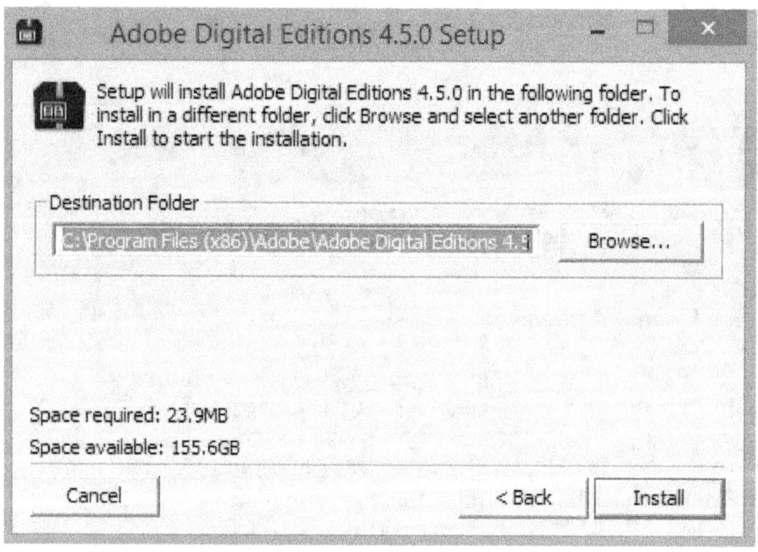

Figure 221. Click the Install button

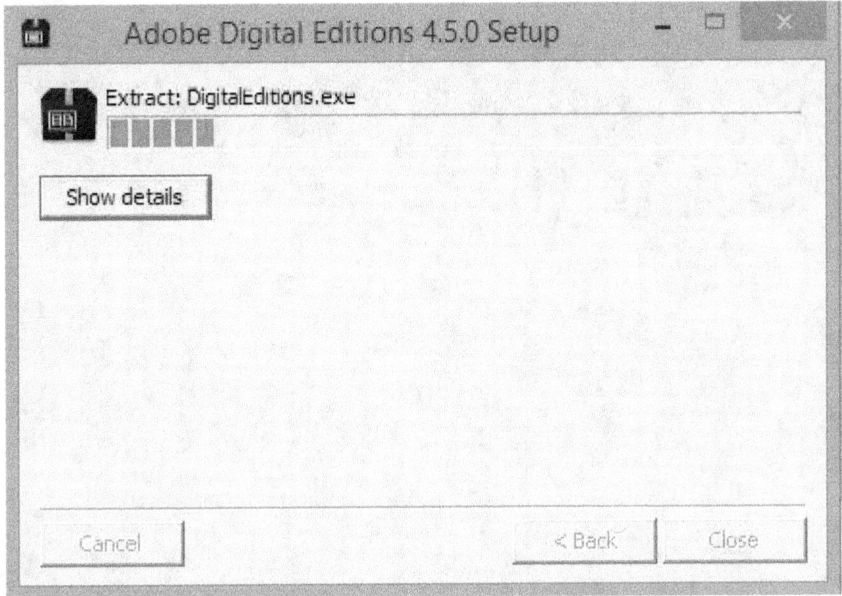

Figure 222. Installation in progress.

Figure 223. Skip the Norton Antivirus installation.

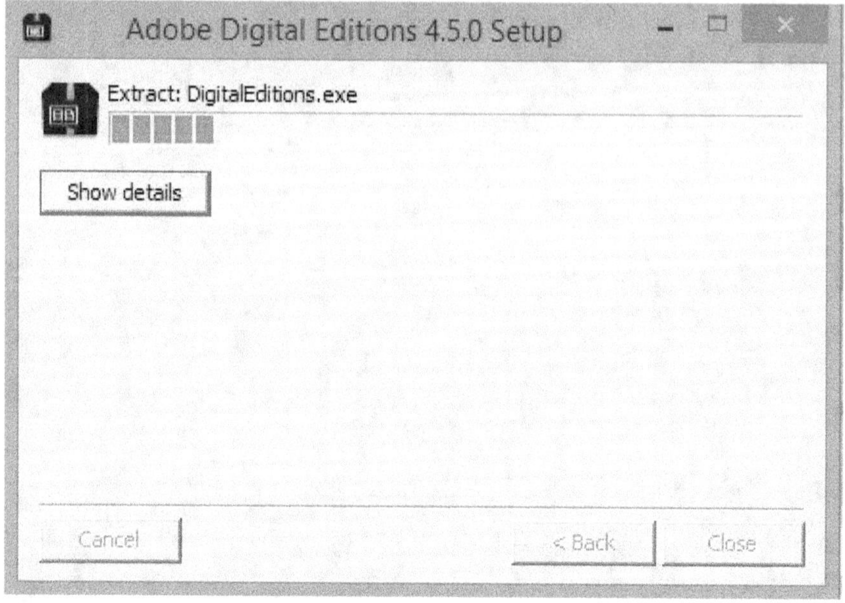

Figure 224. Installation is in progress.

When the Close button becomes active, click it. You are done.
You can download the demo book "Lost in the Fall" from: http://learn-coding.today/epub/fall_en.zip
If you liked the book and found it useful, please write a review. I will be very grateful to you.
If you have no time to format your e-books, and you would prefer that I do it for you, you can send me an email at the email address: support@learn-coding.today
If you need further consultation, you can contact me on Skype.

13. Books by Sergey Skudaev

PHP Programming for Beginners: Key Programming Concepts. How to use PHP with MySQL and Oracle databases (MySqli, PDO)
US: https://www.amazon.com/dp/B008C4JK98US
UK: https://www.amazon.co.uk/dp/B008C4JK98US

C++ Programming By Example: Key Computer Programming Concepts for Beginners
US: http://www.amazon.com/dp/B00EUSMTUW
 UK: https://www.amazon.co.uk/dp/B00EUSMTUW

Learn SQL By Examples: Examples of SQL Queries and Stored Procedures for MySQL and Oracle Databases
US: http://www.amazon.com/dp/B009PD6A2U
UK: https://www.amazon.co.uk/dp/B009PD6A2U

14. Books by Roy Sawyer

Chemistry for students and parents: Key Chemistry Concepts, Problems and Solutions
US : https//www.amazon.com/dp/B0738P9CHZ
UK: https://www.amzn.co.uk/dp/B0738P9CHZ

The Easiest Way to Understand Algebra: Algebra equations with answers and solutions
US: https://www.amazon.com/dp/B06Y1H1HG3
UK : https://www.amazon.co.uk/dp/B06Y1H1HG3

Geometry for Students and Parents: Geometry problems and solutions
US: https://www.amazon.com/dp/1548076856
UK: https://www.amazon.co.uk/dp/1548076856

About the Author

Sergey Skudaev graduated from the City University of New York with a degree in Computer Science.
Since then, Sergey has been working as a software tester and web developer. He also has over ten years of teaching experience in a foreign University.